PERFECT PHRASES™

for

ICEBREAKERS

PERFECT PHRASES™

for

ICEBREAKERS

**Hundreds of Ready-to-Use Phrases to
Set the Stage for Productive Conversations,
Meetings, and Events**

Meryl Runion with Diane Windingland

New York   Chicago   San Francisco   Lisbon   London   Madrid   Mexico City
Milan   New Delhi   San Juan   Seoul   Singapore   Sydney   Toronto

The McGraw·Hill Companies

1 2 3 4 5 6 7 8 9 10   QFR/QFR   1 6 5 4 3 2 1

ISBN   978-0-07-178382-8
MHID   0-07-178382-2

e-ISBN 978-0-07-178383-5
e-MHID   0-07-178383-0

McGraw-Hill books are available at special quantity discounts to use as premiums and
sales promotions or for use in corporate training programs. To contact a representative,
please e-mail us at bulksales@mcgraw-hill.com.

This book is printed on acid-free paper.

Contents

Foreword

"Awkward and painful." That's how a brilliant friend and colleague described her recent experience at a professional meeting. She didn't know anyone sitting around her and was clueless about how to *break the ice*. Her reluctance to initiate conversation caused her to avoid even making eye contact. Retreating inward, she missed out on potential networking relationships all around her. Here was someone who has so much to offer anyone lucky enough to engage in conversation with her yet she remained silent.

These people keep me up nights. I need a resource to give to them—as well as to those who do know how to break the ice but don't know how to do it in purposeful ways or to keep the connection going. In other words, I need a simple resource that combines the wisdom of both introverts and extroverts to help people launch meaningful discussions with people they don't know. And that's exactly what this book is.

Don't get me wrong. I have hundreds of ice-breaking resources on my shelves. So what's different about this one? Most of the available "icebreaker" books are about getting teams and groups to get to know each other to break the tension in the room. *Perfect Phrases for Icebreakers* is focused on interaction more than activity. Plus, the chapters are designed so that each interaction is purposeful. It also has plenty of icebreakers for one-on-one conversations as opposed to most books that are group focused. All of that makes this book relevant and fun to use in almost any situation.

With this book, you have a stockpile of well-considered and effective icebreakers at your fingertips. You have sure-fire approaches to break the ice with any group. You can create synergy and connections that lead to better productivity, innovation, and knowledge sharing.

Your networking ability matters more than ever before. *Perfect Phrases for Icebreakers* will give you the confidence and tools to start conversations that will lead to amazing connections. Get ready to use them. The world is waiting to meet you.

Sarah Michel, CSP
Author of *Perfecting Connecting:*
A Guide to Mastering Networking
in the Workplace

Preface

Well begun is half done. That ancient wisdom applies to many things, including conversations. People are engaged by and often remember your very first words best. However, we often wrestle with those very first words, the icebreaker phrases, the most.

People agonize over how to start certain conversations and meetings. As a speaker on interpersonal communication topics, I am often asked, "How do I start this conversation?" I have effective methods and phrases that I know work. In fact, the collaboration on this book is the result of a relationship that started by my reaching out to Meryl Runion with icebreakers.

My icebreakers have served me for many years, but after collaborating with Meryl, I have so many more to choose from. And now you do too, in this practical book, *Perfect Phrases for Icebreakers*. It offers hundreds of ready-to-use new phrases for almost every business conversation, meeting, or event. If you want to get your conversations and meetings off to a good start, engage people immediately, and increase the probability of productive results, you can discover just the right phrases in the following pages. You can become a phrase master.

Meryl Runion is a phrase master. If coming up with phrases were a martial art, Meryl would be a tenth-degree black belt. I guarantee you will experience several "aha" moments as you read through the phrases. "Aha, that's what I want to say!" Or, "Aha, that phrase will go over so much better!" I had those very thoughts as I read through the phrases and contributed my own.

It has been an honor to see a master phrase creator at work and to be a contributing author on this book. Now, when people ask me how to start business conversations and meetings, I have an easy reference tool for them—this handbook of phrases that they can use immediately, whatever their situation.

Read on and begin some great conversations!

Diane Windingland

Acknowledgments

My first thanks go to Sarah Michel, whose early support kept me from declining this opportunity. Sarah quickly embraced the project in a way that showed me the need for and opportunity in it. Her collaboration helped frame the project in its initial stages. Sarah is all about connecting, and you can learn about her at www.perfectingconnecting.com.

Being the professional networker Sarah is, her clients wouldn't leave her alone. The project focus changed and Sarah's role in this project shifted. Still, Sarah's initial input and encouragement were pivotal, and I am honored that she wrote a foreword for it.

The next key player in the formation of this book was Jarla Ahlers. As the book changed directions, I called Jarla to tap into her vast experience as a facilitator. Jarla's main focus is restorative mediation, and she immediately detailed into the need for icebreakers to get meetings started purposefully. She, our friend Judith Light (whose expertise is in Appreciative Inquiry), and I met for many hours, tossing around ideas and trying to find a structure and framework to guide the process. If you've ever tried to create a structure out of air, you can imagine how tedious that initial development was. Sarah, Jarla, Judith, and I endured it and broke through to new levels of clarity.

I invited Diane Windingland into the process early on. Her level of input kept increasing until she started suggesting and writing some phrase sections on her own. While I edited them to match my voice, Diane's input helped tremendously with the heavy lifting of this book's creation. Diane's involvement took her from being a contributor to earning authorship status. It's a tribute to the purpose of this book that it did. We know each other through Diane's steady and skillful use of icebreakers with me. Her first book is called *Small Talk, Big Results: Chit Chat Your Way to Success!* She practices what she preaches.

Last but by no way least, thanks to Sharon Campbell, Lee Beaumont, and Angela Thompson for their reviews, edits, and excellent contributions. Each has his and her own angle that added insights and phrases that I never could have come up with on my own. They each made this a richer book.

Introduction

This is a book of icebreakers and openers. It's about breaking the ice with people you don't know and with people you do know. It's about breaking the ice with individuals and with groups. If you're looking for a great way to start a conversation, open a dialogue, and get things going, this is it.

The icebreakers are in a phrase format. Everything is stripped to its essence. It's all about what to say when you need to break the ice with a statement, question, observation, or activity.

This book organizes the phrases based on who your conversation is with, what your conversation is about, where you're having the conversation, what you want to accomplish, and what method you're using, that is, how you like to break the ice.

Many of the phrases are ready to adopt as is. Others are ready to be adapted to your circumstance. Chances are you won't open a conversation with someone you just met with an activity like Two Truths and a Lie. But who are we to say? We're sure somewhere in the world someone has successfully done just that. So Diane and I leave it to you to cut and paste, pick and choose, and make the phrases your own. They are here to help you get your conversations and communication off to a good start.

I resisted this topic initially. I thought icebreakers and openers were superficial fluff. I wanted to dive directly into the meat, the heart, the "important" deep stuff in every conversation. I was kind of like a gal or guy who wants to skip past the first several dates, or the salesperson who asks for the sale right after saying hello.

I had a good reason for my disdain. I'd been to events where precious meeting time was squandered in small talk that earned the label "small," and events that were opened by mindless activities intended to help us get to know each other but fell far short of the goal. I saw icebreakers as time wasters. And they can be. But they don't have to be.

Eventually I discovered that well-crafted openers and icebreakers work like preparing the soil before planting seeds. All seeds grow better in well-tended soil. All plants need time to grow. Openers and icebreakers prepare the soil for the growth of productive discussions, collaborations, and relationships. Where you start and how you start influence the entire conversation more than we tend to think.

The Opening to a Book about Openings

You are reading the opening of a book about openings. The words here set the stage for everything that follows. If we did our job well, what you read created a pleasant expectancy and receptivity for the ideas and phrases in this book. If the opening bores you, you're likely to think of more important things to do, like playing Farmville or reading everything in your spam folder. Whether it's the written or spoken word, beginnings matter—a *lot*. Diane and I are writers as well as professional speakers and trainers. We spend extra time on opening words. If you make presentations, I'm sure you do, too.

For meetings and one-on-one conversations, it's no different from written and formal presentations: the beginning sets the tone. Those people texting while you speak—are they texting about how brilliant what you're saying is? Or are they distracting themselves and tuning you out? A good opening gets attention. A great opening makes people forget that they even have a phone to text on.

Openers don't need to be long, clever, or even memorable. But every opener matters.

Your First Step Matters Most

Think about a field of freshly fallen snow. The first steps across it make the most noteworthy impressions. Think of your first words in a similar way. Your opening suggests a direction, your intent, or both. Your second step is shaped by the first.

Some people make absolute, cryptic pronouncements such as, "You never get a second chance to make a first impression." And, "You have 3.5 seconds to get someone's attention." There is some truth to those remarks. If you get off to a bad start, you'll spend time recovering that could have been spent moving the conversation forward. But it's not that absolute. In fact, an authentic recovery can create a bond that might not have been formed without the flub-up. People know how human we all are, and they don't expect perfection. There is a lot more room for do-overs than some people indicate. So, let up on the pressure—but do plan.

The New World of Business Relating

The phrases in this book are current to the times. Our workplaces are different from what they once were. You need conversation starters and icebreakers that work in the new world of business relating. What are some of the differences?

■ We're busier than ever. In fact, I find that few people realize how overcommitted they are. They agree to things they can't deliver—simply because they haven't caught up with themselves. Our openings and icebreakers need to break through the clutter that comes with committing to more than anyone could possibly do.

■ We're multigenerational, international, and very diverse. We need to speak inclusively and adapt our styles from the very first word. That doesn't mean you need to lose your sixties or nineties references, but it does mean that you need to understand that some of the people you talk with weren't where you were as a teen. They might think that those who were there are . . . different.

The same goes for the cultural icons of the twenty-somethings. If that's you, go ahead and use them, but be aware that some people will think anyone who says "totally" repetitively or "shut the front door" sounds like a neophyte or just plain odd.

■ We're virtual. We don't just break ice face-to-face now; we break virtual ice and build rapport remotely more than ever before. Now our words must carry a message that our body language used to. Conferencing helps, but so much of our exchange is written communication where our words do it all. Subject lines in e-mails are a new form of openers and icebreakers, just like the opening words of this book and the first thing you say at any meeting—virtual or otherwise. Emoticons just don't say what tone and body language say in person.

■ We're multitasking and mobile. Unless you're face-to-face or video conferencing, you can't assume the people you're talking to are sitting at a desk focusing on you. They might be broadcasting your words to a room full of colleagues, they might be driving, they might be slicing vegetables, or they might be trying to beat the computer in some new game they downloaded. Or all of the above! And if you are face-to-face, they might be taking notes on what you say or they might be texting someone, pretending to listen to you.

All of these trends add up to the fact that we have more ways to not be present than ever before. Our challenge is to draw our listeners from whatever they're paying attention to toward what we want them to pay attention to—and to do it with our first words.

Purpose-Driven Icebreakers Trump the Trite

We've all been at meetings and events that applied openers and icebreakers designed to build rapport that left us wanting to run screaming from the room. Some seem downright offensive. "If you were an animal, which one would you be?" Puleese!

Of course, you might find great meaning and purpose in that same opener that I use as an example of triteness. And there is a fine art in the inspired use of a banal opening. The key is to know what you want to accomplish and choose your icebreaker or opening with considered intent.

Yes, getting people talking is a useful objective. But simply getting people talking in general, when instead you could get them talking with focus, is a wasted opportunity. You might tie your icebreaker to the meeting topic. You might not. Whether you do or don't, be conscious of your specific intention. What are you trying to accomplish with your opener? State your purpose if it might be useful to your outcome.

The Power of Preparation

We like spontaneity and authenticity. We also like effectiveness and success. Craft an opening icebreaker that requires you to reflect on what you want to accomplish and why. That reflection actually prepares you to be spontaneous and authentic. It also will give you a foundation to adapt as the circumstances suggest, demand, or require. Preparing an opening is a great start to preparing for the entire conversation or meeting.

Extroverts Don't Own Ice Breaking

There's a myth that ice breaking is the domain of extroverts. Give extroverts an icebreaker and they're off and running. However, when I design a specific icebreaker, I'll ask an introvert to help. By definition, it takes a bit more to get an introvert to engage. While breaking the ice comes more easily for an extrovert, it is a hard-won skill for many introverts. Someone who struggles with a skill is often more aware of the nuances of the skill than a "natural." Plus, many introverts demand more substance than extroverts and think an icebreaker or activity that isn't tied to an outcome beyond random mingling is a waste of time. It's a high bar to clear. When an introvert tells me what would get him or her involved, I know I've got an effective option.

Great icebreakers and openings take the attention to the story behind the story—the experience under the surface. They expose the inside story. Introverts tend to inquire into the inner workings naturally. So I love the extroverts in my life. But I don't believe extroverts own ice breaking, and you shouldn't believe that either.

The Effectiveness of Perfectly Phrased Questions

You'll find a lot of questions here. What's so great about questions? Why do questions make powerful icebreakers? Why do we include so many questions in this book?

Questions draw the listener in. It's not by accident that the word *question* contains the term *quest*. Just by posing a question, you send your listeners off on a quest, get them traveling on yours, or create a joint journey. Questions access different parts of the brain and different kinds of intelligence than statements do. For example, you can phrase questions to access visual, auditory, kinetic, or sensory intelligence, such as "Can you picture that?" (visual); "Does that ring a bell?" (auditory); and "How does that feel?" (kinesthetic). Questions can send listeners to places in their past or to places in their imagination. Questions can short-circuit an obsessive thought pattern and take your listeners to greater creative potential.

When you explore possible questions, you start on your own quest. And that quest takes you away from an all-knowing teacher role with all the answers. It also takes you out of a parent role, turning everyone else into children. It transforms you into a colearner or cocreator and invites sharing and creativity. Even if you don't use questions as icebreakers, just by considering questions, your own mindset shifts to a more open perspective.

Questions come with cautions. As any judge who accuses a lawyer of leading a witness can tell you, questions can be misapplied. They can manipulate listeners or audiences to come to biased, predetermined conclusions. They can be used to get people to show their hand before you show yours, so you can use their disclosure to your advantage. They can intimidate when posed aggressively. They can sound like an interrogation even if they're sincere. If you get any sense of a question causing someone to retreat or close down, open up yourself or back off to give the person room.

How to Use This Book

You don't have to read this whole book, although you might want to. Use the table of contents to locate the section that best applies to your needs and find your phrase immediately. Some of the phrases are statements, some questions, and others set up activities.

Generally the beginning phrases in each section are more directed toward individual conversations. Individual phrases are marked with a simple bullet: ●.

The middle phrases in each section tend to be more directed toward group conversations. Phrases that generally apply to groups are marked with a diamond: ❖.

Activity icebreakers offer interactive dialogue or guide some kind of action. They're marked with a movie clapper: 🎬.

Again, the distinctions are general, not absolute. For example, you might find some useful stand-alone phrases in the activity groups or group phrases that could be used with individuals.

We divided this book into sections according to whom you're breaking the ice with, what you're speaking about to break the ice, where you're breaking the ice, why you want to break the ice, and how, or what approach you use, to break the ice. Look through the table of contents, see what stands out to you, and go there.

The true gold in this book comes from considering the thinking behind each phrase. When you select a phrase, ask yourself the following questions:

- What am I trying to accomplish with this phrase?
- Why did I pick this phrase?
- Is there a way I could improve on this phrase for my purposes?

Not only will those three simple questions help you use the phrases in this book to your best advantage, but they also will help you understand the situation with greater clarity, which will increase your effectiveness throughout the entire conversation.

This book is for you to apply in any way that serves your needs. We're here to help, so contact us with questions, contributions, and ideas: merylrunion@speakstrong.com and diane@smalltalkbigresults.com.

SECTION

WHY: Purpose-Driven Icebreakers

B egin with the end in mind." You've heard it before. But what does that mean for icebreakers? It means two things: First, know what you want the conversation or meeting to accomplish. Second, based on that, know what you want your *icebreaker* to accomplish. These phrases will help your icebreaker do the heavy lifting of opening your interaction or meeting in a way that will lead to the desired outcome.

Note that this section contains many more phrases intended for groups, marked with a diamond, ❖, than many other sections. It also contains many phrases to start activities. Those are marked with the movie clapper symbol: ▰ .

Perfect Phrases to Highlight the Conversation or Meeting Topic

What is the meeting about? The meeting organizer can publish a meeting PAL—statement of purpose, agenda, and length, and use a topic-centered icebreaker to focus attention on the conversation or meeting subject. That way you'll be talking about the same thing.

- Thanks for meeting with me. I'm curious, why did you accept my offer to meet to discuss (topic)?
- What interests you about (topic; example: social media)?
- How long have you been (studying, using) (topic; examples: organizational change, social media)?
- When you (saw, heard, discovered) what this meeting is about, what thoughts did you have?
- ❖ Who was told they had to be here today?
  - → What went through your mind about the topic?
- ❖ If you created an e-mail subject line about this topic, what would it be?
- ❖ Why have you come to this meeting? What brought you here?
- ❖ We're here to talk about (topic; example: leadership). I find that means a lot of different things to different people.
  - → What does it mean to you?
  - → How do you define (topic; example: *leadership*)?
  - → How does your perspective on the topic differ from most people's?

❖ What do you want to explore about (topic)?
  → What do I need to know about (topic)?
  → What about (topic) lights a fire in you?
  → What do you know about (topic) that other people don't know?

Perfect Phrases to Uncover Assumptions, Desires, and Expectations

Do you need to know what people want? What people know? What people expect? Well, ask! Use an icebreaker to uncover assumptions, desires, and expectations.

● I'll cut to the chase. What can I do for you?

● I know why I'm here. I'd like to know why you're here. Can you tell me what you hope to get out of this?

❖ Imagine you have a magic wand. What would you like to change by the end of the (conversation, meeting)?

🎬 Let's go around and fill in the blank.
  → One thing I'm hoping to learn today is _____.
  → One thing I find confusing is _____.
  → One thing I'd like others to learn today is _____
    _____.

🎬 What are your outcomes and objectives for this (conversation, meeting)? Please write the answers to these questions.
  → What is you fondest, dearest wish for today?
  → What are you hoping to get out of today?
  → What would make this discussion a success for you?

→ Let's go around and share our objectives.

→ Did you notice I asked the same question three different ways? That's because different ways of phrasing questions evoke different responses. I really want you to walk out of here with what you came for.

→ What will you contribute to the success of this session?

▰ I'm going to role-play something. Ready? (Stomp in the room, slam the door, sigh heavily, throw a book on the table, and peer at the group).

→ Describe what just happened?

→ How do you know that's what happened?

→ What part of what you described is objective? How do you know?

→ Did you directly observe that?

→ What did you directly observe?

→ How many of you found it difficult to separate your observations from your interpretation of your observations?

→ How common is it for us to make assumptions without realizing we're doing it?

→ How can we keep from doing that today?

Perfect Phrases to Get People to Focus on Outcomes

There are times when banter, small talk, and tangents are useful. Other times, it's distracting. When the conversation or meeting needs to maintain a strict focus, these opening phrases will help.

- As much as I enjoy checking in before getting down to business, today we need to focus if we're going to (outcome; example: create an action plan.)

- Let's start by picturing ourselves walking out of this meeting happy with what we did here. What did we accomplish?

❖ Let's stay focused on our task of (purpose) today. We have a lot to accomplish, and I'm committed to our finishing on time.

❖ We only have time for half an icebreaker today. ☺ That will leave us (30 minutes) to review, brainstorm, and decide what to do.

❖ Let's go around the room and speed share names today. Then we'll turn our brains like lasers to (focus).

❖ We can visit and stay late, or we can focus and get out of here on time. I'd love to visit, but I know my priorities. How about you?

❖ We chewed on these topics extensively last meeting. Today we are here to decide. I expect this to go quickly.

❖ There are a lot of issues we could talk about. Today we need to focus on (topic). If we get off track, we'll mark and park the tangent and get back on track. The tangents we'll address later.

❖ Who wants to get out of here on time? We can—if we stay focused.

❖ If any of us smells a tangent, let's bring it back to focus on the outcome. It's not being rude; it's being efficient. So plug your nose if you smell a tangent and we'll refocus.

🎬 Let's break into groups of three. Each group is tasked with deciding what you want to get out of this (meeting, event). Pick a leader to present the desired outcome according to your group.

→ Let's hear what others had to say.

→ How did your group reach consensus?

→ Now go back to your groups, and see if any of your outcomes have changed from what other groups said.

→ Now decide what each of you intends to do to make sure you get what you came for.

→ Did being asked to take action to ensure your outcome change anyone's desired outcomes?

→ What kind of actions did you come up with?

Perfect Phrases to Build Rapport

Have you ever had someone get down to business too quickly? Kind of like you're all a bunch of machines instead of people? How'd that feel to you? A simple icebreaker designed to build rapport can grease the wheels for subsequent communication. These phrases create a quick sense of commonality, relationship, and trust.

● Finally we meet! I've really been looking forward to putting a face to your e-mail address!

● I wanted to meet with you because we both care a lot about (topic; example: the success of this project).

● I've really been looking forward to this meeting and talking with you about (topic)!

❖ Who else had been curious about what it would be like to actually meet in person?

 → I hope I look the way my voice sounds!

 → Do I look like my e-mails?

❖ Have you ever experienced (some common experience that you are having; example: technology not cooperating)?

❖ We'll be working with new technology today, so this might take a group effort. Who brought a sledgehammer?

❖ What did we do the last time we were in this situation that really worked?

❖ We didn't create this situation (example: this economy) but we're in it together. I can't think of anyone else I'd rather have on my team for support in a situation like this.

❖ We have different roles in this project, but let's start by defining our common commitment.

 → Why do we care about this project?

 → What are we all committed to doing here?

🎬 Let's start by sharing a motto, a phrase or saying that you live by. Something like: "Say what you mean and mean what you say without being mean when you say it." That's one of mine. What mottos do you like?

🎬 Let's begin with everyone asking their neighbors their name, what they came to learn, how they see (situation), and what expertise they bring. Be ready to share what you learn.

 → We'll start with (name). Please introduce your partner, his or her perspective, and his or her expertise.

 → (Name), it's payback time. I mean, time to reciprocate!

We're going to tune in by matching and adding to actions. I'll start by patting my head. The person on my right then will pat his or her head and add a new motion. The person on the right of that person then will mimic the first two motions and add his or her own—and on and on. Got it? Here goes.

→ How many did we complete?
→ Did you find it fun, frustrating, or both?
→ Who had a strategy they used to remember that could be useful to the rest of us?

Perfect Phrases to Inspire Collaboration

Survival of the fittest is programmed into us in many ways. We often unconsciously take adversarial stances. Open in a way that invites—and involves—collaboration.

● We have a choice. We could argue and negate each other to defend our own positions, or we could listen and discuss different perspectives in ways that support each other and move us forward together. I know what my choice is.

● I suspect we have two things in common: we haven't been looking forward to this meeting, and we want to make things work for both (all) of us. Am I right?

● We've been at odds on (issue). What will it take for us to work together?

● I regret not having this conversation sooner. I think we've been working at cross-purposes and we need to work together.

❖ Have you ever had a situation where everyone worked together like magic?
  → What made it work?
  → Why did it feel like magic?
  → What can we apply here from that?

❖ What do the phrases "looking out for each other" and "having each other's back" really mean?
  → When have you experienced that before? Please be specific.
  → What helped create that kind of collaboration?
  → What kept that kind of collaboration from happening?

🎬 I need one person who favors (one option you're meeting to discuss) and one person who favors (an opposing option).
  → Sit across this table from each other. Get in arm-wrestling position. Now go!
  → OK, we'll go with the winner's idea. Makes sense, doesn't it?
  → Of course we wouldn't make an important decision by arm wrestling. However, that's what we're doing when we let the most aggressive person or the person with the loudest voice overpower the reasons behind our options.

🎬 Let's think of ourselves as the guardians of each other's success here.
  → What does that mean to you?
  → What would you like for it to mean to the people on your team?
  → Are there systems in place that get us working as adversaries when we need to work cooperatively?

→ Let's do a quick exercise. Turn to your partner.
→ Partner A, make a fist. Show your fist to Partner B.
→ Partner B, see that fist? Try as hard as you can to open your partner's fist.
→ Now switch. Partner B make a fist. Partner A, try as hard as you can to get your partner's fist open.
→ How many of you were able to open your partner's fist without resorting to tickling or bribery?
→ How many of you thought to ask your partner, will you please open your fist?
→ And those of you who had your fist closed, what were you holding on to? What kept you from being the guardian of your *partner's* success and allowing your partner to open your fist? Were you looking out for your partner or just looking out for yourself?
→ Now, I set this exercise up to trigger competition. I confess. And you still had the choice to work collaboratively. Let's applaud those of us who worked collaboratively. Now let's applaud the rest of us for demonstrating the normal response to this situation.

First, I'd like each of you to write a work-related challenge, problem, or area you'd like to improve on the top of the sheet in front of you. For example, "How can I build rapport among team members who have never met?" Then pass your sheet to the person on your right.

→ Now take 60 seconds to write possible solutions to the challenges that are passed to you. I'll time you and tell you when to pass again.
→ Pass! (Continue.)
→ Does everyone have his or her own sheets? Please take two minutes to review what you have.

→ Tell us what ideas you like that people offered.
→ Let's use each other as resources to handle our challenges.

🎬 We'll start with an activity to build teamwork. Without talking or mouthing words, please line up according to how long you've been working here.
→ What did you do that worked?
→ What could you have done to be more efficient?
→ Did someone take a leadership role? How did they do it? Was it useful?
→ I didn't give a lot of direction. What interpretive decisions did you have to make in implementing?
→ How'd we do as a team?

Perfect Phrases to Pique Curiosity in Your Message

Can you think of a time when a speaker or author had you sitting on the edge of your chair wondering where he or she was taking you? A teaser can be a great way to start a meeting or conversation. You can open with a statement or remark that leaves your listener(s) wondering what's coming. Use words like "what if" and "surprises." Here are a few icebreakers to hook your listeners' curiosity.

❖ What if everything you know about (topic; examples: communication, mold, sales) is a lie? I'm going to tell you something today that will surprise you.

❖ Would you like to create a future distinct from the past? We're going to discover a way today. Well, it sounded good at the Tupperware meeting I attended. . . . And I actually think it's possible.

❖ I realized the reason why we're here isn't the one I originally thought it was. More on that later. Now I'll proceed with the original agenda.

❖ This isn't going to be a routine meeting. You'll learn something unusual. But first, let's lay the groundwork.

❖ If you ever wondered about (topic; example: how they slice hot dog buns when they are joined together in the package), you're in the right place. Really! I'll explain later.

➔ If you never wondered about (topic), you're about to wonder why you never wondered about it.

➔ I thought I knew about (topic; example: design software), but then something happened that showed me how wrong I was. But first . . .

❖ You're about to become an expert in a topic most people know little about. And that tells you how little most people actually know about it!

Perfect Phrases to Expand Limited Mindsets

Life consists of contradictions, opposites, and ironies. It's easy to get locked into one side of the equation or the other. For example, "Look before you leap" sounds prudent, yet there are many who would counter by saying, "He who hesitates is lost."

Conflict is often a result of being stuck on one side of a polarity. Directly addressing contradictions, ironies, and oddities is both intriguing and useful for helping people expand limited mindsets.

● Let's imagine our customers are sitting at the table with us as we talk today.

▰ Let's look at common truisms that seem to contradict each other, such as "out of sight, out of mind" and "absence makes the heart grow fonder." You name some, and I'll list them.

→ How can maxims that contradict each other be true?

→ What kind of seeming contradictions do we face at work?

→ How can we resolve these?

▰ Let's list oxymorons. That includes things like "a fine mess," "act naturally," "bittersweet," "burning cold," or "chaotic organization," "deliberate error," "executive decision," "pretty ugly." You get the idea.

→ How do seeming opposites like this actually make sense?

→ Where are you living or working with seeming opposites and making it work? I can name an example: my marriage! You?

▰ In "The Allegory of the Cave," Plato discusses the lives of a group of people chained in a cave who can only see the outside world via the shadows reflected in the flickering firelight. From this they deduce what the outside world is like. Everyone is in kind of a cave. I am a (white woman, black man, etc). That is one of my caves. We're all human beings on the planet earth. That is our collective cave. Our worlds are full of caves.

→ Tell us about a cave you work or live in.

→ If you live in a very different cave from other people, how does that affect how you hear what they say?

→ What caves do we work in here?

→ Who should we consult to get perspectives we are missing in our caves?

→ How can this cave allegory help us hear people's words in a different context?

→ Now imagine one person escapes and sees the outside world, then comes back to the cave to tell the others what she or he saw. For me, it's a bit like what happens when one of us attends a powerful conference and tries to share the experience. What would you relate it to?

→ Do you think the cave residents believed him or her?

→ Why or why not?

→ What could she or he do to persuade them?

→ Do you have a mental block against people who return to your cave with new information?

→ How can you break that mental block?

Perfect Phrases to Transform Resistance

Many of the martial arts, like tai chi, redirect the opponent's force instead of resisting it. The goal of good martial artists is to not have to fight. They dissolve, redirect, and transform opposition in ways that keep it from escalating.

● I've heard the best defense is no defense at all. I know we're on opposite sides of (issue). I'd like to hear what you have to say without me defending my situation at all. Are you willing to talk about it?

● The best way out of a mess is through it. I'd like to sit side-by-side with you, looking at the issue together, and walk through it with a mutual goal of getting to the other side. Are you open to that?

▰ Some say the best defense is no defense at all. Find a partner. Partner A is the person with the most jewelry on.

→ Partner A, think of an issue that bugs you. It could be traffic, someone who doesn't follow through—anything that gets under your skin. Got it? The only thing is, if your issue is with your partner, choose another one. I'm going to ask you to complain to your partner without trying to be fair. Am I clear in my explanation?

→ Now Partner B, you'll listen and respond with resistance. Turn your partner's complaint back around on him or her. Say things like, "It's your fault" and "This wouldn't be happening if you . . . "—that kind of thing.

→ Partner A, how did you respond to the resistance? Did it fuel your frustration?

→ Now, A, you're going to complain about the same thing, but this time, B—you'll respond with phrases that acknowledge your partner's complaint without agreeing with them. Use phrases like, "I understand how you might feel that way." "I can see that is a huge issue for you." And, "I might feel the same way if I were in your shoes." Ready? Go!

→ Partner A, how did that feel to you? Did you like having your complaint acknowledged?

→ Partner B, was it easy enough to use the phrases to acknowledge your partner without agreeing?

➔ OK, now A, you're going to do the same things as before, but this time I want you to blame your partner. Think of all kinds of reasons why your complaint is his or her fault. Say things like, "I blame you for . . . " and "Here's what's wrong and why I blame you for it." Got it?

➔ Now Partner B, you're going to respond by resisting in the same way you resisted the first time your partner complained. Make sure your partner knows how wrong he or she is.

➔ A, how did that work for you? Did any of you almost find yourself believing it really was your fault?

➔ One last time. Partner A, complain to your B again, and blame him or her for everything, the same way you did before. Partner B, this time you're going to respond by acknowledging your partner's complaints without agreeing with them. Say things like, "I might feel that way too if I were you." Ready? Go.

➔ B, did you find it harder to acknowledge your partner's complaints when he or she was complaining about you?

➔ Can you see how being able to acknowledge someone's perspective without agreeing with it can be a useful first step in transforming resistance?

🎬 Stand up and face your partner. Partner A, ask your B a simple question, such as, "Do you like ice cream?" or "Are you driving home after the meeting?"

➔ Partner B, answer "yes, but." Follow your yes with the word *but* and a comment. For example, "Yes, but I can't eat it" or "Yes, but I can't go until I finish work on a project."

→ Keep asking questions until I tell you to stop.

→ Partner A, how did that feel when your partner kept "yes-but-ing" you?

→ Now, A, same thing only B will respond with "yes, *and*" plus a comment. For example, "Yes, I like ice cream, and I haven't had much lately" or "Yes, and I'll leave right after I finish work on a project." Ready? Go!

→ Partner A, how did you feel when your partner used "yes, and" as a response?

→ How can we use this in discussions and arguments?

→ What is the attitude difference between the two phrases?

Perfect Phrases to Inspire People to Share Resources and Support

Do you have colleagues and team members who operate like adversaries instead of allies? Even among functioning teams, people can unthinkingly hold back necessary information, resources, and requests. These opening phrases are designed to spark a spirit of sharing and support. Use words like *team*, *help*, and *together*.

● I'll start by asking, how can I support you in your work?

● Sometimes people come to me for help (example: with their conversations). I know people come to you for (example: software tips). I'd like to combine resources.

● I'm here to help you succeed. I see our success as interdependent.

● I'm a resource in this project. Here's some of what I offer.

● What do you do best? I'll tell you what I'm good at. (Example: I'm great at developing phrases.) Your turn!

❖ This will come as a shock to you, but I can't do this alone. And I don't expect any of you to do it alone either.

🎬 In a perfect world without any budget or other constraints, what kind of resource(s) would you want that you don't have now?

→ Pick a resource. What barrier keeps you from getting that resource?

→ What about that resource makes it important?

→ Is there another resource that can circumvent that barrier?

→ Who else might have that resource who would share it with us?

🎬 We aren't here to compete. We are here to *complete*. And it will take all of our input to complete this project.

→ What do we need to complete this project?

→ Who has the specific resources or expertise that we listed to complete this project?

→ How might competing keep us from completing what we set out to do?

🎬 Harry Truman said, "It is amazing what you can accomplish if you do not care who gets the credit." I agree—*and* I like giving credit where it's due.

→ I have a list of things I'd like to acknowledge you for.

→ Let's start by everyone giving credit to those who have made our work easier.

■ Let's break into groups and make a list of skills and resources in each group. Some starter phrases are:

→ What skill or resources do you have that people don't ask you to share as much as you might wish? For example, I'm good at creating systems and find many of the processes people create aren't as efficient as they could be.

→ What about your work inspires you? For example, I love finding great new ways to say things.

■ Take a minute to write three things you need help with in this project. Then list three things you can support others with. After that, we'll share our lists with the group.

■ To dramatize how much we depend on each other and how connected we all are, I have a ball of string. (Name), take one end and hold it, and then throw the ball to someone you depend on for support.

→ (Name 2), please hold on to the string and toss the ball to someone you depend on for your success. (Continue.)

→ Now let's talk about why we chose the person we did to toss the string to.

■ I'd like for each of us to make a list of the tools we have in our toolbox and use to do our jobs. This can include software, hardware, and techniques. Ready? Go!

→ Who else is using a tool you use?

→ How could you help each other use those tools?

→ Which tool would you *not* want to be without?

→ Does anyone else have a tool that you aren't using but that could be useful?

🎬 Turn to your partner. If you're on the left, you're Partner A. Say this to your partner. "If I were to advise you, not that I am, what do you think I'd say?"

➜ Partner B, respond with your best guess.

➜ Partner A, let your partner know if he or she was close or not.

➜ Partner B, respond by saying thank you. It's your call whether you want to follow up later. Now we'll switch.

Perfect Phrases to Get People Asking Good Questions

If you want people to ask good questions to get all the confusion on the table, these phrases will break the ice in ways that inspire inquiry.

● If you had to explain (topic) to your next-door neighbor, what questions would you prepare to be able to answer?

🎬 I'd like to play Three Questions today. When I make a point, I'll invite you to ask me three questions about what I said. They don't have to be good questions. The point of the exercise is to get you asking, so your real questions will rise to the surface.

➜ Let's practice by asking three questions about the Three Questions game I just introduced. Someone start the process with a question about how Three Questions works.

➜ Did any of you discover you have questions you didn't think to ask?

➜ How can you use this technique on your teams?

🎬 To get ourselves into a questioning mode, pick a partner. We're going to ask each other a series of questions. We'll have a moment for a quick answer, but don't worry too much about the perfect response. The point is to get in the habit of asking questions. Then I'll ask the group some questions.

→ First, ask each other a *who* question, such as, "Who do you report to?"

→ Next, ask each other a *what* question, such as, "What do you do best?"

→ Next, ask a *where* question, such as, "Where will you start on the project?"

→ Next, a *when* question, such as, "When did you start working here?"

→ Now, a *why* question, such as, "Why do you like your smartphone?"

→ Finally, a *how* question, such as, "How can we improve our process?"

→ Who found themselves wondering about things they didn't know they wondered about?

→ What was the most useful thing about the exercise?

→ Where did you get stuck, if anywhere?

→ When did the exercise click for you, if at all?

→ Why might this be a useful exercise?

→ How can we improve on this exercise?

→ Who besides me thought the exercise was pretty awesome?

🎬 We're going to start with supporting each other by asking questions. Everyone pick a partner, and then pick a challenge you have. Something that bugs you: meetings that start late, people who don't return calls—that kind of thing.

→ Got it? Great. Now, the person with the darker shirt on goes first. Share your challenge with your partner. Partners, just listen.

→ OK, partners, now ask your partner a question that starts with *who*, such as, "Who could help you with this?" or "Who does it impact?"

→ Great. Now ask your partners a question that starts with *what*, such as, "What might happen if . . . ?" or "What would you like to see happen?"

→ Now ask your partner a question that starts with *when*. For example, "When does this matter?" or "When do you need to move forward?"

→ Next, ask a *where* question, such as, "Where would you like to start?" or "Where could you get help?"

→ Now, ask a *why* question, such as, "Why does this keep happening?" and "Why do you care?"

→ Excellent. Finally, ask a *how* question. For example, "How could you get help?" or "How do you plan to start?"

→ My next question is for the people with the challenge. Your partners didn't offer any advice. Was the dialogue helpful anyway?

→ What did we learn from this that will help us succeed in this project?

→ As we proceed, I invite you to notice any confusion that remains and ask questions to get the answers you need.

Perfect Phrases to Initiate Spontaneous Interaction

Have you ever left a conversation or meeting thinking that the structure got in the way of genuine exchange? Some meetings and conversations need to be highly structured and focused. Others are more exploratory. These phrases will help you set the stage for a free-flowing conversation to discover possibilities that might not emerge in a more directed and structured interaction. Use words like *imagine* and *explore* to spark creative thinking. Note that most of these phrases can be used to open both individual and group conversations. We marked them with the symbol that indicates the category we see them as most useful for—but don't let that limit you!

● What would you like to (explore, discuss, experience) today?

● I deliberately didn't set an agenda for today. If you have a burning issue, we can talk about it; otherwise, I was thinking it could be a great use of our time just to chat.

● Let's approach this conversation with expectancy rather than expectations—kind of the sense that anything could happen.

● What different conversation could we have today?

● Is there anything you were hoping would happen at this meeting? Any topic you wished would come up?

- Let's explore what happens if we just talk without a goal. It might take us to some surprising places.

- We're always so purposeful with each other, which is great. Today, before we get down to serious business, let's pretend there's a watercooler in the middle of the room and we're talking around it.

- Where would you like to see us go today?

- I'd like to discuss possibilities we could explore that we haven't yet. Any thoughts?

- What have you been thinking about (topic; example: the way the work flows) that you haven't said out loud? Anything?

❖ Sometimes the most productive meetings are those that meander through a meadow of ideas, concerns, issues, and possibilities. Put on your hiking boots, and let's head out. There is no wrong path today. Future meetings, yes. Wrong path, no.

🎬 Let's go around the room and fill in the following sentence stems.

   → Imagine a meeting where we talked about _____ . Fill that in with a topic.

   → Great, now, fill in this one. One thing I'd like to explore that we haven't is _____ .

   → OK, now try, If we weren't always under deadline, I'd like to talk about _____ .

   → Anyone hear a topic that they'd like to actually discuss?

Perfect Phrases to Encourage Engagement and Participation

People often need encouragement to get involved more deeply. For example, when I work with collaborators on phrases, they often need nudging to create their own phrases since they see me as the expert. Whether it's a conversation or a meeting, use phrases that let people know their input is both welcomed and encouraged—phrases that get them participating in spite of themselves!

- I can get lost talking about this, so if I do, please jump in.

- I'm so glad we're finally talking. I'm more interested in what you have to say than to hear myself speak, so interrupt me freely!

- Today we'll assume the only bad question or idea is the one we don't express, OK? It's about openness.

- Have you been imagining anything about (topic; example: our vision) that you haven't said out loud?

- I know you're newer to (skill; example: phrase creation) than I am. Don't let that hold you back from contributing. Anything you say helps me understand what you know. Your contributions can show me where I'm not clear. And I'm so close to the topic that you will see things I miss.

- ❖ Today you get a playing card for every meaningful contribution you make. The person with the most cards at the end of the meeting gets a prize.

❖ Today, I'll be asking for some volunteers to do some activities. I really appreciate when volunteers help out, so I pay my volunteers. In chocolate.

❖ I promise you, if you volunteer to come up I won't embarrass you! Scout's honor!

🎬 I'm giving out words to each of you. They are words like (example: reframe, optimize). Another person has the same word as you do. That person is your competition. When you hear me say your word, exclaim, "You said it." The first person in a pair to note me saying their word gets a point.

➜ No tricking me into saying your word!

➜ Now we know who's paying attention.

➜ Who finds this exercise useful for focusing your attention?

➜ Who finds you're so busy listening for a word that you miss the point?

Perfect Phrases to Encourage Openness, Authenticity, and Airing Concerns

How open do you want people to be? Is there such a thing as too much openness and authenticity? Well, there is such a thing as inappropriate disclosure. But open and authentic communication is about dropping pretense and posturing, and speaking to the need of the moment. That's always a good thing. Communication doesn't need to be "touchy-feely" to be authentic and valuable.

Words like *truth* and *honesty* can be useful, but use them with care, because they can evoke their opposites. It is usually better to create a fertile soil for openness than to ask for it directly. Here are some phrases.

- I want nothing to come between us and the truth, including—or especially—my ego!

- I like it when people agree with me, and I like it even more when they're honest with me. If you can do both, great. If you can't, I'll go for honesty.

- ❖ I know this will be a shock to many of you: I discovered that some of us—well, actually all of us—make mistakes. It also may surprise you to know that I see it as an indication that we've moved out of the predictable zone into the learning zone. And that's a good thing.

- ❖ I have a confession to make. It's about a mistake I made this week. I could hide what happened, and no one would know. But then you wouldn't have the benefit of learning from my folly.

- ❖ Who made a mistake they learned from this week? And just to be clear, we promise to respond in ways that won't leave you thinking that sharing your mistake was your biggest mistake.

- ❖ I'm feeling a bit overwhelmed with all we have ahead of us. Is anyone else feeling that way?

- ❖ We'll never get ahead by pretending things are what they're not. So let's fill our water glasses halfway, and toast to a half-empty *and* half-full look at things.

❖ Think what you would say if you could say anything at all about (topic)?

➜ How far is that from what you plan to say?

➜ What holds you back from being completely open?

❖ Let's be like the ancient alchemists. Let's take lead and turn it into gold. If you've got an idea or comment you suspect will go over like a lead balloon, we'll find the gold in it.

❖ Here's the deal. If something's not working for you, let us know what and suggest how we can fix it. If something really melts your butter, let us know what and suggest how we can leverage that idea. Sound like a plan?

❖ Am I the only one who has concerns they'd like to address?

❖ What conversation do we need to have about (topic)?

🎬 Let's break out into pairs. Your mission is to talk about anything in the world without using the word *I*. Ready?

➜ How many of you were able to do it?

➜ Why do you suppose it's so difficult to avoid using the word *I*?

➜ How can this exercise help us work together as a team?

🎬 We're going to open by playing a game called Things That Are. I'll start with a quality, then we'll go around and fill in the category. For example, I'll start with Things That Are . . . Difficult. I'd say catching all my typos is high on that list. Let's go around.

➜ Next, let's play Things That Are Fun. Designing fliers is on my list. Let's go around on that one.

➜ OK, Things That Are Irritating. (And so on.)

Perfect Phrases to Initiate Feedback

Feedback is information. That's it. Without it we can't progress. And yet the very idea of feedback can put us on the defensive. Some people recommend "feedback sandwiches"—tell someone what you like, then detail how messed up the person is, and conclude with an element of praise. (Of course, feedback rarely is really about how messed up you are, but it often comes across that way.) Here are some icebreakers to initiate smoother, more effective feedback. (Note, many of the phrases in this situation are multipurpose.)

- The purpose of this meeting is to provide feedback. Feedback is essential to learning and improving. Are we ready to start?

- Are you open to some feed-forward? Yeah—I had to think about that a bit when I first heard it myself.

- I'd like to review what happened and why, so we can learn from our experience and repeat the things that worked and improve the things that didn't go so well. It's more of a feed-forward session.

- I'm not here to criticize you. I'm here to support you. That means pointing out opportunities for improvement.

- This (meeting, conversation) is an opportunity to give and receive feedback. I'll receive first. I want to know what you see me do that gets in my way or your way or hurts the project—and what you'd like to see me do instead!

● It's tempting to suggest that everything is perfect as is and avoid the discomfort of identifying problems. That would be a huge loss to us both.

● I see a lot of potential here. That's why I want to focus on what isn't working in order to see how we can maximize the potential. When we identify it, we can do something about it.

● We have a lot of problems to address here. Before we start, I want to point out that we expect problems. If we didn't have any, we'd know we're playing it too safe.

● I find it easier to give feedback on how to improve good work than poor work. Keep that in mind as I point out some improvement opportunities in your work.

● I have a couple of observations about what happened. Are you open to hearing them?

❖ Let's review our progress as if we cared. Oh, wait! We do!

❖ Let's assume that we're all committed to excellence when we offer feedback. Keep that in mind both when sharing and when receiving feedback. That's what it's all about.

🎬 Some groups have hot seats. We have opportunity seats.

→ Any thoughts about what the difference between a hot seat and an opportunity seat is?

→ Which sounds more inviting?

→ Which sounds more useful?

→ The opportunity seat is where we share feedback about what works, what doesn't work, and what the next step toward excellence would be. Who'd like to go first?

Perfect Phrases to Initiate Creative Brainstorming

Got a problem to solve? Need ideas? Break the ice in ways that get people focused on discovery. Use words that inspire creativity and discovery, such as *imagine* and *possibility*. Here are some phrases for you.

● We need fresh, new ideas to deal with this situation. So, let's play!

● I have some ideas. You have some ideas. Let's put our heads together and see what we discover. We'll probably both be surprised. We need fresh, new ideas to deal with (situation).

❖ We need some ideas on (challenge; example: how to track manpower). The goal of this activity is to generate ideas about (challenge) and *only* to generate ideas. Later we'll evaluate, but for now, instead of saying "yeah, but" say "yes, and." Nothing is too wild.

🎬 Imagine us reflecting back on this moment a year from now, congratulating ourselves for having handled our challenges so well.

→ Now, envision what steps we took to get there.

→ Is anyone surprised by their own imaginings?

🎬 This is a creative brainstorming session, so let's start with some creative brainstorming about what makes creative brainstorming work.

→ Who has an idea about how we can generate ideas?

→ What makes it safe to be creative?

→ How do you like people to respond to your ideas?

→ How do we build on ideas without sounding like we're negating them?

→ Let's make this real time. We'll start with the first person who contributed. Let's look at how people responded. You suggested (suggestion). I took notes on everyone's responses. They are (notes). Which responses stand out as being helpful to the creative process?

🎬 I'm handing out cards for you to write an idea that would improve our (situation; example: team organization) that's too far out or too radical to really do.

→ Let's go around and read them. When we're done, I'll ask some questions.

→ Were any of these ideas actually doable?

→ What was the craziest idea? Can you imagine it ever being feasible?

→ What ideas do these ideas inspire in you?

Perfect Phrases to Add Levity to a Conversation or Meeting

Have you ever had a conversation with someone who was a master of buzz kill? Someone whose first words sucked the light, air, and life out of the room? Levity creates openness. A message expressed in a lighthearted way is often more likely to get through than the same message communicated "in all seriousness." We're not talking about being dismissive of or minimizing problems. We're not talking about hiring a clown before you announce layoffs. Clearly, every situation has its ideal level of levity. But even a message as heavy as unexpected layoffs will be more palatable if presented with optimism. Before you select one of these phrases, weigh it (pun intended) for its levity. Don't be afraid to be goofy.

- I read that (meetings, conversations) are more productive when everyone lightens up a bit. That's why I ordered a canister of helium. Seriously, folks . . .

- I read that (meetings, conversations) are more productive when everyone lightens up a bit. Please begin by depositing loose change, key rings, and purses weighing more than five pounds in the middle of the table.

❖ Does anyone remember why we're here?
  → Oh good! I knew I could count on you!

❖ What is *your* favorite way to make meetings fun? That's not a rhetorical question.

❖ Let's start with the important information everyone wants to know. We escape—I mean, get to go home—at (time). And recess—I mean, breaks—are at (time).

❖ I planned to order healthy food today to cut costs. Then I realized I needed fun food to increase attendance.

❖ Too many (meetings, conversations) have been sabotaged by "terminal seriousity." Let's not do that. Let's get the job done and have fun in the process.

❖ Out of respect for the seriousness of this topic, I'll spare you my dumb jokes. Have you heard the one about the priest, the rabbi, and the minister? You'll be relieved to know you're not going to hear it now either.

❖ I'm (example: Diane, author of *Small Talk, Big Results: Chit Chat Your Way to Success!*) and a fountain of jokes—both entertaining and pathetically lame.

❖ I was told that every (meeting, conversation) starts as a blank sheet that we write on as we feel moved to. That might mean your blank stares are a good thing—for now, anyway.

❖ The reason for this meeting needs no explanation. Therefore, I will explain.

❖ I take this project very seriously. That's why I'm planning on us having fun in our meetings about it.

❖ If this stops being fun, please (example: put a clown nose on). We're here for a purpose, but if it gets too bogged down, it's time to recalibrate. If you have a rubber chicken handy, you're welcome to throw that at me too.

❖ Meetings should be fun. I command you to enjoy this meeting. And to be empowered too!

❖ My name is (example: Lyrem). Actually, it's (Meryl) but I've always been a bit backward. I invite you to be a bit backward too. Please turn to your partner and introduce yourself backward.

🎬 Let's open by sharing something most people don't know about us and then tossing this ball to someone else for them to share a point.

🎬 Please turn to your neighbor and give him or her a silly way to remember your name.

Perfect Phrases to Get Current Since the Last Conversation or Gathering

It's really helpful to know where you are before you move ahead. It helps to catch up those who missed the last meeting and refocus the rest of us. That's why breaking the ice with updates can be an excellent idea. Note that most of these icebreakers can be used in one-on-one conversations and with groups.

- I've been thinking a lot about our last conversation and want to tell you how your words impacted me.

- I know I leave meetings thinking, "Oh, here's what I *should* have said!" If you did that last week, I'd like for you to start us off by sharing your reflections.

- As I recall, you were (something specific). How is that going?

- I know you were facing (specific problem). How did you solve it?

- What's the best thing that happened since we last (met, spoke)?

- ❖ Who has reflections from the last meeting?

- ❖ Have you applied anything from (the last meeting, our last conversation)? What happened?

- ❖ What's different since the last time we (spoke, met)?

- ❖ Check-in time. What's the most significant event in your world right now?

- ❖ Share a win with (me, us).

❖ What have you done better since the last meeting? Any stumbling blocks?

❖ I'll begin with a summary of where we were at the end of our last meeting.

Perfect Phrases to Give a Conversation or Meeting Overview

Do you ever look at a map to orient yourself? That's what an overview does. A great way to start a conversation or meeting is by giving people a road map of the conversation, highlighting where you are, what the bigger picture looks like, and where you intend to go. That context puts your listeners at ease.

● I'm good until (time). What's your schedule? I'd like us to do an overview before we dive in.

● Here's how I see where we are now (brief description). By the end of the discussion I'd like us to be (brief description). I don't know everything about how we'll get there, but the next step is (step).

❖ I love how my PALs help meetings end on time. That's purpose, agenda, and length. So let me introduce you to today's PAL.

❖ Anyone want to get out of here on time? Me too. Here's the plan that will get us out by (time) with the work done.

❖ Let's start with an overview. First, does anyone have a conflict or commitment that might mean leaving early?

❖ Here's the plan. We'll start with (example: a review of our last conversation).

  → Then (example: we'll update each other on what has happened since we spoke last).

  → We'll move on to (the next step) and if we stay focused, we should be out of here by (time).

❖ Last time we met, we agreed to (actions, decisions). I'll update on my assignment. Then we'll hear from each of you.

Perfect Phrases to Learn about People

What would you like to know about the person or people you're going to be talking to or meeting with? Think about it for a moment. You probably wonder what they're like—but what does that mean? You can create your own "I'd like to get to know you" phrases simply by exploring your own curiosity. Even in strictly business conversations, it's both helpful and comforting to have a sense of what makes people tick. Note that most of the one-on-one statements can also be used as an icebreaker for a group.

● I confess, I'm curious about (example: how you got where you are in the industry). Do you mind telling me?

● What one question might an interviewer ask you that would draw out some interesting information about you?

● What talent do you have that you hope to contribute to your work?

- Tell (me, us) something surprising about yourself.
- What (motivates, inspires) you?
- Tell me about the best part of your (job, position).
- What attracted you to this (field, company, job, etc.)?
- What do you like to do in your spare time or for fun?
- If you could study anything in the world to your heart's content for free, what would it be?
  → Are you studying that now?
  → What are you learning?
  → Why aren't you studying it?
- What's the best way for (me, us) to communicate with you or to get your attention?
- What would you like to know about each other?
- What's the weirdest job you ever had?
  → What did you like about it?
  → What did you learn from it?
  → Did it give you any experience that's useful for this team?
- Tell us about a celebration that was particularly meaningful to you, at work or outside.
  → What made it meaningful?
  → What kind of celebrations could we be having?
- Have you ever imagined your fantasy career?
  → Mine is (example: writing nighttime soap operas with a wise woman character who is the voice of clarity).
  → Turn to a partner and describe your fantasies—but no more than a PG rating, please.
  → Who heard a career fantasy that inspired them?

Perfect Phrases to Help People Remember Names

Are there people in your life whose names you can't remember? Does it feel awkward? Knowing names is a basic part of connecting with people. Avoiding someone's name is awkward and creates a barrier. Use these phrases to break the ice in ways that help people remember names.

▰ Let's play a game to help us remember names. Introduce yourself to others by repeating your name to the point of being obnoxious.

→ For example, I'll demonstrate. Hi, I'm Diane, Diane Windingland. Diane Windingland from St. Paul, Minnesota. The Diane Windingland who is leading this session. OK, Diane Windingland says, "Your turn. Go!"

→ Who had a particularly creative way of repeating names?

→ Who had a smooth way of repeating his or her name?

▰ My name is (memory tool; example: Meryl Runion. Meryl is like Meryl Streep. Runion rhymes with onion.) So if you forget my name, think about (Meryl Streep eating onions). That's how I help people remember my name.

→ Your turn. Tell us your name and how we can remember it.

▰ To help us remember each other's names, introduce yourself and tell us something about your name. You could tell us who you were named after, or how your parents picked your name, or what you like or dislike about your name. I'll start. (Example: Leland Beaumont—the land by the beautiful mountain!)

■ We'll open with an activity to help us learn each other's names. I'll start by saying my name. The second person will repeat my name and add his or her name. The third person will repeat the first two names and add his or her own. We'll go until we get lost, and start again with the person who couldn't remember. Ready? Meryl.

→ How many did we get?

→ OK, let's each take a piece of paper and write down every name we remember. We'll see who has the most.

■ Let's play the "name game" to help us remember names. This is a little silly, but it works! Each of us will say a descriptive adjective that starts with the same letter as the first letter of our name and then our name.

→ For example, I am Marvelous Meryl. The next person says, "Hi, Marvelous Meryl, I'm Decisive Diane." The third person says, "Hi, Marvelous Meryl and Decisive Diane, I'm Lucky Linda." And so on.

→ Now let's test our success. I'll toss a ball to someone, and the rest of the group will state that person's name.

→ Now you toss it, and we'll shout out the name of the next person.

→ I hope you all picked adjectives you like, because these adjectives are sticky.

Perfect Phrases to Uncover Strengths and Talents

If the purpose of your conversation or meeting is to find out what people are good at, open with an icebreaker phrase, which draws out their skills . Here are a few.

- I've heard great things about you, and today I get to find out what the fuss is all about!
- Have you done the Strengths Finder assessment?
  - → What are your strengths?
  - → What do you imagine it would tell you about your strengths?
- What would you describe as your greatest strength?
- ❖ We're sitting on a gold mine of talent here. I'd like to make this (conversation, meeting) a modesty-free zone. That's how we'll find out where our strengths are.
- 🎬 I heard about a judge who asked a quarterback on a witness stand how good he really was. The quarterback replied that he was the best quarterback Notre Dame ever had. When his coach later expressed surprise, the quarterback explained that he was under oath. That's the kind of honesty I invite today.
  - → Let's each start today by sharing the quality or achievement we're proudest of on our perfectly tweaked résumé.
  - → If you were under oath and asked to explain what you do best, what would you say?
  - → If you were under oath and asked who benefits from your skills, what would you say?
  - → If you were under oath and asked why the team is lucky to have you on board, what would you say?

Perfect Phrases to Inspire Performance Excellence

No matter how good we are, we can and must continue to stretch, improve, and grow. Striving toward perfection doesn't mean being a perfectionist. It's not about driving ourselves to obtain the unobtainable; it's about moving in the direction of excellence. These icebreaker phrases will help.

- I called you in for coaching, not because you're behind in any way but because you're so good. I want to develop that potential and encourage you to reach high.

- You're performing to job standards. Great job. I called you in to talk about stretch goals—targets to do more than get the job done and to develop your abilities.

- If you had a wish list and could change anything about your job, what would you change?
    → What materials and equipment would you get if you could?
    → What training would you get if you could?

- ❖ Albert Einstein considered compound interest to be the most powerful force in the universe. Continuous improvement is like that. Just a little more knowledge and skill each day is a very powerful thing.
    → Who spends a little time each day improving their knowledge or skills?
    → What has the effect been?

🎬 Everyone please take three pennies and toss them in this basket.

→ Look at where you stood. Did you stand so close you couldn't possibly miss?

→ Did you stand so far away you couldn't possibly hit the target?

→ Who picked a spot that was a stretch without being unobtainable?

→ How does this reflect the goals you set for yourself at work?

→ When are we better off going the route of certainty, and when are we better off stretching?

→ What would happen if you did this every day, increasing the distance by one inch?

→ How could you stretch yourself just a tad every day at work?

→ How could we stretch ourselves as a team?

🎬 I'm passing out cards for you to write job activities that you wish were a part of your job but that you don't have the time, training, or approval to do.

→ Let's go around and share.

→ What can you actually do, based on your list?

Perfect Phrases to Acknowledge Someone Going through Major Change

When a group or individual is experiencing major change, you may choose to address it in your icebreaker. Otherwise, it can be like an elephant in a living room that no one acknowledges.

It's tricky to be sensitive without being intrusive. These phrases will help.

- I heard about (a loss), and I don't know if you want to talk about it or not. I just want to say I'm sorry.
- I heard about (a loss), and I can't imagine what you are going through right now. I am here to support you. Please ask for help any time you need to. In the meantime, would you find it helpful if I were to (specific thing)?
- It seems a bit mundane to talk about (example: budgets) when (you, we) are going through such major change. Still, we do need to focus on our project. So before we dive in to the purpose of this (conversation, meeting), I want to let you know my heart is with you even as we hammer out details.
- I know there's a lot going on in your life. Let me know if there's anything I can do and if we need to talk about it today.
- ❖ I've asked (name) if (she, he) minds if we share the fabulous news. And here it is.

Perfect Phrases to Acknowledge Challenges from Change

Sometimes when things change (and when don't they), we focus on the fires that change creates, the balls that get dropped, and the things we don't know because we've never been where we are now. It's good to remember the big picture: that change can be challenging. These phrases break the ice by recognizing that.

❖ We're going through a lot of changes here. It's happening whether we embrace it or resist it. We might as well be volunteers instead of "voluntolds."

❖ What's the difference between a volunteer and a "voluntold"?
  → Who wins when we step up to the challenge and embrace the change? Who loses?
  → What can I do to help the "voluntolds" become volunteers?

❖ We want to be the leading edge but not the bleeding edge. Where do you see our lead bleeding us?

❖ What do you love about change? What are the challenges?

❖ We're implementing major changes, and while some balls will get dropped in the process, I think we're really on a pretty heroic journey. So before we talk about where we are compared to where we're challenging ourselves to go, and before we examine the dead bodies, let's review how far we've come.

🎬 What words do you think of when I say the word *change*? Let's be more specific than "I don't wanna." I'll write them out.
  → How many of these words are positive? How many negative?
  → How many of these words reflect resistance? How many reflect embracing change?
  → What do you think creates resistance to change? What creates acceptance?

🎬 If we think change is mechanical and overlook the emotional component, we're kidding ourselves. What kinds of emotional responses are you having personally or observing in others we need to be aware of?

→ What kind of emotional responses would be more fruitful?

→ How can we flip our emotional response into a more positive one?

→ What would help (you, us, them) move through those responses quickly?

🎬 I've always heard that change happens when the pain gets bad enough, the promise is appealing enough, and the steps are clear enough. The reward needs to be worth the risk.

→ What pain drives or inspires this change?

→ What's the promise or reward from embracing the change?

→ Who needs help determining the best next step?

🎬 Let's talk about our "yeah, buts."

→ We need to change our way of (process; example: tracking inventory). Now fill in the blank. Yeah, but

_____.

→ Let's go through each "yeah, but" and create a "yes, and."

🎬 People don't resist change; they resist being changed. Please tell your partner about a change you resisted and one you embraced.

→ Looking back, why did you resist the one change?

→ Why did you embrace the other?

→ What does that tell us about change and how we can make it smoother?

Perfect Phrases to Introduce Sensitive Subjects

It's tempting to tiptoe around sensitive subjects. Don't hem and haw or dance around the point, but do take a moment or two and use an icebreaker to prepare everyone for the discussion. Some phrases:

- I'd like your permission to raise a sensitive subject.

- There's no easy way to start a conversation about (topic; example: personal hygiene issues). We do need to talk about it, and I'll listen with my heart. I want us to get through this with our dignity intact.

- There's no easy way to talk about this, so I'll do it the best way I know. Let's not make it any harder than it needs to be.

- I have some things to say that I imagine will be hard to hear. I think it's important that you know, and that's why I want to have this conversation.

- This is one of my least favorite parts of (example: managing). I'm tempted to tiptoe around it, but that wouldn't serve either one of us. So here's the deal.

- I wish I had better news to give you. I'll tell you straight out, answer your questions, and explore next steps with you.

● This is a difficult conversation, and I'll need your help and your indulgence as I fumble through in an attempt to talk about it honestly and delicately.

● This is a tough topic to raise, especially with someone whom I consider a friend.

● We need to have a conversation that could be uncomfortable for both of us. Know that I want you to feel safe to respond honestly and openly to our conversation, and I'll do the same. The goal here is to communicate and find a mutually agreeable solution if possible.

❖ We need to talk about (sensitive subject). Before we dive in, I'd like to ask, what can I do that might make the conversation easier for us?

🎬 Who here has a *former* friend?

→ Here's what can happen. There's something we need to talk about, but there's never a good time to raise it. And we wonder if we might be overreacting, so we let it go. And then there's another issue. And before we know it, we're avoiding that person completely. We need to be able to talk about sensitive subjects to have healthy relationships.

→ Find a partner. Partner A, say this to Partner B: "There's something I've been reluctant to talk with you about." Go.

→ Partner B, respond by saying, "That tells me we need to talk about it." Go.

→ Partner A, say, "I don't want to hurt your feelings." Go.

→ Partner B, respond by saying, "I'm an adult. I can handle your sincere communication." Go.

→ Partner A, say, "I don't know how to say it." Go.

→ Partner B, respond by saying, "You can practice with me."

→ Partner A, say, "I could be wrong."

→ Partner B, say, "Your perspective helps me understand you. I won't judge it to be right or wrong."

→ Partner A, say, "I don't want to lose our friendship."

→ Partner B, respond by saying, "If speaking sincerely can wreck our friendship, it wouldn't be much of one."

→ Partner A, you just practiced five of the lame excuses people give to avoid discussing sensitive subjects. Partner B, you gave your partner the reason it was lame.

→ Next time you want to avoid a sensitive conversation, name the lame excuse. It will help you overcome your hesitation.

SECTION 2

HOW: Method-Driven Icebreakers

A re you a story teller? A punster? A wanna-be stand-up comic? How do you like to break the ice? These phrases will help you hone your ice-breaking approach of choice.

Perfect Phrases to Break the Ice with Questions

Questions are a great way to break the ice—if your inquiry is genuine and you're not intrusive. Ask yourself what you sincerely want to know about the other person. Often you'll find there are more questions you want to ask than you imagined. Here are some question icebreakers. Note: you'll find many more uses of questions to break the ice in the section "Perfect Phrases to Break the Ice by Getting People Asking Good Questions."

● Do you have any icebreaker tips for me? You seem like a natural. I'm learning how to do it.

● I'm so excited you're here because I've been wanting to ask you . . .

🎬 We're going to break the ice with questions today. I'll pass out a list for you to ask each other. Here's an overview.

→ What's new in your life?

→ What have you learned today?

→ What kind of car do you drive? How did you pick that car?

→ What was an influential event in your life?

→ What's your favorite place on the planet?

→ Name a pet peeve.

→ What makes your day?

→ Have you had a celebrity sighting?

→ Tell me about your first job.

→ What's the most courageous thing you've ever done?

→ What's the most challenging thing you've ever done?

→ What have you learned to do that was difficult at first but is easy now?

→ What are you currently working to get good at?

→ What do people learn about you after they've worked with you for a while?

→ What do you wish people would ask you about?

🎬 We're going to mingle by asking questions. Find a partner. The taller one will go first.

→ If you're first, ask your partner a yes-no question. You can ask about anything, such as, "Do you ride a motorcycle?" or "Do you use PowerPoint in your work?" If you get a yes, keep asking questions.

→ When you get a no, the person answering will become the person asking.

→ Switch partners and repeat the process.

→ Who found themselves picking obvious "yes" questions?

→ Who asked questions that could have gotten a yes or a no?

→ How often do you choose questions by anticipating the answers?

→ When is and isn't it appropriate to gear our questions by the likely answers?

Perfect Phrases to Break the Ice with Humor

Humor makes for a light beginning. Avoid humor at anyone's expense—except possibly your own. If you're new to humor, don't start with jokes. A little light humor is lower risk. With light humor, if no one thinks your humor is funny, it won't be so obvious. Here are a few humorous phrases to get you started.

❖ After many requests, this meeting is . . . being held anyway!

❖ At this meeting I want you to speak openly about your concerns. To make sure we don't miss anything important, listening devices and hidden video cameras have been strategically placed around the room. Now, tell me everything!

❖ How many of you are here to contribute your ideas? How many of you are here to share information? How many of you are here . . . for the free food?

❖ I have no problem admitting I'm wrong. Admitting I'm wrong to other people is a huge challenge to me! Ready to watch me struggle?

❖ I want to hear what you think. But first, let me give you a piece of my mind. Wait . . . I don't have a piece to spare! Got some spare brain cells?

❖ I've read that the average person falls asleep in seven minutes. In meetings it's two. Just so no one falls asleep in this meeting, we'll conduct it with everyone standing. Just kidding. I'll do my best to keep this meeting moving along.

🎬 We're going to do things a little backward today—literally. We are going to talk about solutions before problems. That's right. Pick a problem in your mind. Don't tell anyone. Got it? Write down your best solution.

　→ Now pass the solutions to me.

　→ I'll read your solutions out loud, and we will try to guess what the problem is.

Perfect Phrases to Break the Ice with Self-Disclosure

It doesn't always work this way, but generally if you share more of yourself with someone, that person will share a little more with you. Here are some phrases.

● I'm excited and nervous about our conversation today.

● I was so excited about this meeting that I didn't sleep much last night. My brain was overflowing with ideas, and when the sun came out, some of them actually made sense.

❖ I did some research to figure out how to start this discussion. Then, I put my books down and shut down my computer. I decided the best place to find the right words was inside my own heart.

❖ Today's topic matters a lot to me because (heartfelt reason; example: I once was on a team that failed because we couldn't collaborate). I'm not dialing anything in—I care about how this discussion goes.

❖ Remember when meetings involved pads of paper and brand-new pens for taking notes? I miss those days. Nobody was texting then!

❖ I speak to all kinds of groups, and this one makes me nervous because (reason; example: it's a new culture to me, and I'm sure I'll put my foot in my mouth).

Perfect Phrases to Break the Ice with General Observations

People often don't see what's right in front of them. Drawing their attention to aspects of the situation or environment can help focus their attention. Plus, it's a shared experience that can build rapport.

❖ What a good-looking group! What? It works for Leno and Letterman!

❖ Isn't it amazing how many more people show up to meetings when food is involved?

❖ I notice you're all sitting by department.

❖ I like the way you've made yourselves comfortable in the room.

❖ You're all pretty quiet!

❖ You're pretty lively!

❖ Is there anyone here not texting?

❖ What other observations can we make about ourselves before we begin? Let's focus our attention in the room.

❖ The fact that you all came in on a Saturday tells me how important this topic is.

🎬 Did you notice (example: the new curtains)?
  → Without peeking, describe the ceiling.
  → Don't peek. Who can tell me what kind of shoes I'm wearing?
  → In case you haven't guessed, this isn't about the curtains, the ceiling, or my shoes. It's about setting mental distractions aside and being fully here.
  → Without peeking, what's the agenda today?
  → So let's shift our attention to the agenda.

🎬 Make a list of everything on a penny.
  → Which way is Abe looking?
  → What words are on it?
  → Does it say, "In God We Trust"?
  → Is there a date on it?
  → Did any of you get the word "liberty"?
  → The point of this is, we often stop seeing things that we see every day.

🎬 Please face a partner and observe him or her.
  → Now, turn your backs to each other and change four things.

→ Face each other again, and see if you can tell what changed.

→ How did it feel to be studied that way?

→ (After responses) How many of you went right back to the way you were before you made the changes?

Perfect Phrases to Break the Ice with Introductions

Introductions are excellent opportunities to break the ice and build rapport. A little extra thought and really good icebreakers can leverage the introduction opportunity. You'll find more introduction icebreakers throughout the book.

● Hi. I'm (your first name). That's (your first and last name). If you forget, please ask me to repeat it.

● I see you're new here. I'll introduce you around. What shall I say?

  → Is there anything the team should know about you that you'd like me to tell them?

  → Is there anything you'd rather tell them yourself?

  → I'd like to champion you here. What would you like for me to say to do that?

🎬 Please write a nickname you have, have had, or would like to have, on an index card. Then pass the cards to me. I'll read the nicknames, and we'll guess who belongs to what nickname.

🎬 I'm passing out index cards. Please write a personal hobby or interest, and pass it to me. I'll read the hobbies, and we'll guess who has which hobby.

Please write a list of three creative questions to ask some-one you're just meeting.

→ Now, let's trade, and for the next five minutes, please circulate and ask each other the questions on your list.

→ (Name), let's start with you. Please stand up.

→ Who has met (name) already?

→ What did you learn about (him, her)?

→ How did it work for you to ask a question someone else chose?

Let's break into pairs to interview each other.

→ You have three minutes to learn about each other. Here's fair warning: you'll be asked to introduce your partners to the group as a whole. So be sure your part-ner hears what you want the group to know!

→ Some possible questions are what expertise they bring to the project, what they came to learn, why they do what they do, and what motivates them.

→ Let's go around the circle and introduce our neighbors and what we've learned.

→ Introduce your neighbor as his or her champion. Talk about the person in a way that shows what an asset he or she is to the team.

We're going to go around the circle and introduce our-selves. To mix it up, if your birth date is an odd date, intro-duce yourself like you're delighted to be here. If your birth date is an even date, introduce yourself like you'd rather be anywhere else but here.

→ (As people share) What do you think, odd or even?

→ Now let's introduce ourselves a second time with a little different information and switch our enthusiasm level to the opposite of the last time.

→ Which style introduction built rapport?

→ How can we use this experience to keep the rapport level high in our working relationship?

🎬 I'm passing out cards for you to write an interesting introduction to yourself on. Write anything that paints a picture of who you are, not what you do.

→ Now, I'll draw one at random and read it.

→ Point your finger in the air. On three, point to the person you think this is. Ready? One, two, three!

→ Why did you pick the person you did?

→ How creative were the descriptions?

→ What did we learn about (name) we didn't know before?

🎬 Let's form a circle.

→ I'll start by tossing a ball to Jasmine. Jasmine, when you catch it, say "Thank you, Meryl." I'll reply by saying, "You're welcome, Jasmine."

→ Then Jasmine tosses it to someone else and repeats the process.

Perfect Phrases to Break the Ice with Business Cards and Name Tags

Business cards and name tags give us clues about each other that we can leverage into icebreakers. The key is to pay attention and note any curiosity that arises.

❖ I like your business card! Who designed it?

❖ Nice business card case! Where did you get it?

❖ We'll start by putting the name of someone we admire on our name tags.

🎬 Let's play Two Truths and a Lie. On the back of your business card write two things we don't know about you and a third thing you've made up.

→ Put your card in this box.

→ I pulled out one from (name). (Read.) Who thinks the first is the lie? The second? The third?

→ What did you learn that you didn't know before?

🎬 Let's make our name tags more interesting!

→ Put your favorite quote on your name tag.

→ Put your hometown on your name tag.

→ Put your favorite hobby on your name tag.

→ Put your favorite book, movie, or song on your name tag.

→ Write the name of a professional journal or blog that you like on your tag.

→ Now let's circulate and read each other's tags.

→ Who got a valuable conversation going with that icebreaker? Tell me about it.

Perfect Phrases to Break the Ice with Listening Phrases

Listening isn't waiting to talk. True listening is not a passive activity. Here are a few phrases to break the ice by talking about listening and setting the stage for listening.

❖ Think of a time when you felt really listened to.

→ What made you feel listened to?

➜ How did that level of listening affect you?

➜ How can we listen to each other better today?

❖ Think of a time when you didn't feel listened to.

➜ What did the other person do that left you thinking he or she wasn't listening?

➜ Did the other person say anything that implied he or she hadn't listened?

➜ How else could you tell the person wasn't listening as well as you wanted?

🎬 Let's list the qualities of great listeners. I'll write them out.

➜ What do great listeners look like?

➜ What do great listeners do that poor listeners don't do?

➜ How can you tell they're listening?

➜ Are there surprises on the list?

➜ Would you agree that we all pretty much know what to do to listen well?

➜ Then what's the difference between a good listener and a great listener?

➜ Is it skill or the choice to apply what skills we already have?

🎬 I'll open by reading a few paragraphs from an article on our website. (Read.)

➜ I prepared 10 questions. (Ask questions. After people answer each question, give the correct answer.)

➜ How'd we do?

➜ Now I'm going to read another paragraph and ask you another 10 questions. But, this time, the person who gets the most answers correct gets the chocolate. (Read)

➜ Here are your questions. (Ask questions.)

→ How did our listening improve when we knew we were going to be tested?

🎬 Now find a partner. Pick one person to be Partner A and the other to be Partner B.

→ Partner A, describe your home to Partner B.

→ Partner B, describe Partner A's home back to him or her.

→ How'd that go?

→ Now, do it again, except, Partner A, you can describe your office to Partner B. And then Partner B will describe the office back to Partner A.

→ What did we do differently once we became aware that we were going to be held accountable for our listening?

🎬 We're going to play telephone. I'll start by whispering something to the person on my right. If there are any speech readers (lip readers) in the room let me know now so I can give you your own instructions.

→ Now pass the message around the circle.

→ (To the last person) What did you hear?

→ Let's do this again, only this time we'll confirm what we hear. After I whisper to you, please whisper it back and we'll keep talking until we're sure we have it.

→ Now we'll pass the message around the circle the same way.

→ What difference did confirming the message make?

→ Did any of you think you understood the message and discovered that you didn't really?

→ What kind of messages do we need to do this level of confirmation for?

Perfect Phrases to Break the Ice with Appreciation

We all like to be seen and acknowledged. People often wonder if other people respect their gifts, service, and contributions. These phrases will help break the ice with acknowledgment.

- It's humbling to talk with someone who's done what you have.

- It's a privilege and an honor to spend this time with you.

- Great job on (success). How did you get the idea to do it that way?

- I want you to know, even if I don't say it enough, that I appreciate your (hard work, contribution) to (project, achievement).

- Thank you for pulling together to get the project back on track. I know it was hard work.

- Gracias, merci, mahalo.

- (To a large group, looking left, right, center) Thank you. Thank you. Thank you.

▰ We've come a long way and are ready for a new challenge, but it would be criminal to move forward without stopping to acknowledge how far we've come. I don't want to do anything criminal!

   → Let's go around the room and repeat this sentence, filling in the blank: If I weren't so humble, I'd brag about how I _____.

   → Let's go around the room and repeat this sentence filling in the blank: If I were under oath and had to testify about what we did well, I'd say _____.

▮ Pick a partner. The person on the right, I want you to spend the next three minutes telling your partner specific things you appreciate about yourself. Go.

→ How many of you found that easy?

→ How many of you ran out of things to say?

→ How many of you wanted to qualify your appreciation, such as giving an example of a time when you messed up?

→ Who found themselves respecting their partners the more they heard about their finer qualities?

→ What benefit could come from being able to talk gracefully about our strengths and skills?

▮ Let's take a few minutes to focus on what we're doing well. Pick a partner. The person on the right, I want you to spend the next three minutes telling your partner what you did well on this (project, job). After three minutes, I'll tell you to switch.

→ What did we learn?

→ Now let's go around the room and repeat this sentence, filling in the blank: One thing my partner (name) has done well is _____.

Perfect Phrases to Break the Ice with Interest

Interest is one of my favorite ways to break the ice with people. All of us are interesting if we take the time to step back and really see who we are. The best source of interest icebreakers is your own curiosity. Here's a tip: make a list of 20 possible questions to ask different people in your life. You might discover how much you don't know that you would like to.

● What was it like for you to _____?

● Are you as (happy, confident, enthusiastic, etc.) as you appear?

● What's the most courageous thing you've ever done?
  ➜ What gave you the courage to do it?
  ➜ Did you consider bailing?
  ➜ How did it change you?

● If you could do (achievement) all over again, what would you do?

● Tell me about your (family, work, hobbies).

● How long have you (worked, lived, volunteered, been a member) here?

● How did you learn how to do what you do?

● What do you enjoy doing when you're not working?

● Fill in the blank. One thing people find interesting about me is _____.

🎬 Find a partner. Now, Partner A, tell Partner B: "I'm interested in learning more about *blank* from you" and fill in the blank.
  ➜ Partner B, do the same.
  ➜ Two more rounds.
  ➜ Now just talk freely. You can talk about things you had expressed interest in—or not.

Perfect Phrases to Break the Ice with Stories

People like stories—if they're relevant and short. Here are a few ways to break the ice with stories.

- Would you share the story behind (example: the book you wrote)?

- There's a story behind (example: why I'm in this business). Do you want to hear it?

- There must be a story behind that (refer to an interesting accessory).

- You make success look so easy. Do you have any stories about times when you weren't sure you were going to make it?

- I'd like to hear about the challenges your team faced to get here.

- Can you tell me about some of the obstacles you faced and how you overcame them?

❖ The good news is, I'll start this meeting with a story. If you don't like stories, the good news is, it's short.

❖ I have a long story about (topic of meeting) and a short one. I'd like to share the short one. A funny thing happened on the way to this meeting . . .

🎬 Let's open by updating each other in a short-story format. I'll start.

→ The coffeemaker was empty, so instead of making more coffee, I settled for tea. I knew my team was depending on me, and I wanted to respond to their e-mails before they got in. I looked up at the clock and took a sip. (And so on.) Your turn!

🎬 Our brand tells a story. Who will tell it today? Start with, "Once upon a time . . ." (Example: Once upon a time there was a woman who was so used to going along to get along that she didn't know how to speak up when she had to. She developed an entire system of powerful communication called SpeakStrong.)

🎬 Who can make up a story on the spot? How about a part of a story? How about a word of a story?

➜ We're going to make up a group story one word at a time. I'll start. The next person will say the next word of the story. Ready? Yesterday . . .

➜ Now we're going to do the same things with a new guideline. Be boring and unoriginal.

➜ One more time. This time we'll go phrase by phrase. Choose phrases to make the person before you look good.

➜ What was different between the first and third stories?

➜ Did you ever want to control how someone followed up on what you said?

➜ If the third story was better than the first, why was that?

➜ What if we all focused on helping each other succeed? What if no one ever showboated? What would that do for the team?

🎬 We're going to toss a ball, and the person receiving it will speak a random, simple, descriptive phrase. It could be something like "the quick brown fox" or "took too long."

There are no wrong phrases. I'll start. "It didn't take much." Catch—your turn!

→ You guys are great! Now, we're going to do the same thing, but this time when we catch the ball, we'll speak a phrase that relates to the one that went before. Then we'll start a new phrase and toss the ball to someone who will speak a phrase that relates to what we just said. I'll demonstrate with (name).

→ Great. Which round was easier? More interesting?

→ Which felt more like storytelling?

→ How can we use this to help us share our stories with each other in ways that don't sound pedantic?

Perfect Phrases to Break the Ice with Activities

If you haven't realized it already, this book has activities dispersed throughout each phrase section. If you don't find an activity you like here, check the sections that relate to whom you're communicating with, what you're talking about, where you need to break the ice, and why you need to break the ice—that is, what you want to accomplish. The activities are toward the end of each phrase section. Below are just a few of our phrases for activities.

🎬 We're going to practice honoring our own message in the face of indifference. Stand up and find a partner. The taller person is A.

→ Partner A, talk about something that you're passionate about to your B. Keep talking until I say stop. Ready? Go!

→ Great. How did that feel?

→ Now, find a new partner. A, you'll share the same story, but this time, Partner B will respond by saying "so what" and walking away. A, follow B and continue to talk without interruption.

→ How did that feel? Who found it more difficult to stay connected to your passion around the topic? What thoughts were you having?

→ Do you ever need to insist on being heard? Are you willing to do it in the face of disinterest?

▄ Let's stand in a circle. I'll start by pointing at someone. That person will point at someone else. That person will point at another person, and so on until everyone has someone pointing at them and is pointing at someone.

→ Now, stand still and look at the person you pointed to. That person is your role model. Any time your role model does anything, imitate it. If your role model shifts his or her weight, coughs, or anything, imitate it.

→ What happened? Why weren't we just standing still?

→ Who started the movements? Are you sure? Ask (him, her).

→ How does this relate to real life? How can we use it to stop negative cycles?

→ Let's say someone wants to spread gossip with you. How could you stop gossip from spreading?

→ How can we use this in a positive way?

▄ We all have different comfort zones. To demonstrate this, stand five feet away from your partner. Partner A, take small steps in until you feel like you're at a comfortable distance for chatting.

→ Partner B, move in until you find your closest level of comfort. Then move in another inch.

→ OK, now one or both of you is uncomfortable with your partner's proximity, right?

→ Who is feeling a bit irritated with their partner?

→ Did any of you respond by moving back?

→ One of you, politely request that your partner stand back just a bit.

→ Whose partner asked in a graciously assertive way? What did he or she say?

→ Thank your partners and sit down.

 We're going to play different roles for the first part of the meeting. You have cards that determine your role.

→ Hearts are advocates. Your mission is to point out what's right about the information I present.

→ Clubs are opponents. Your mission is to point out what's wrong about the information.

→ Diamonds are the "yes, and" group. Your mission is to affirm what you like about the information and add new ideas.

→ Spades are the "yes, but" group. Your mission is to find things you like and things you don't like.

→ Aces and Jokers are wild. You can play any role you want. (Introduce the agenda and start with the first item.)

→ Aces and Jokers: did the roles others played influence the one you chose to play?

→ Who felt expanded by their role?

→ Who felt limited by it?

🎬 We're going to practice giving directive feedback. I need a volunteer.

→ Close your eyes. I'm placing a basket for you to toss coins into. After every attempt, the audience will offer you feedback to help you get closer on the next toss. Here's your first coin to toss.

→ Let's give (name) feedback about how to get closer next time.

→ (Name), what feedback worked well for you? What didn't work as well?

→ How can we use this to improve how we offer feedback to each other?

🎬 I'm going to pretend to be an alien. I've never put on a tennis shoe. I am depending on you to guide me. I can't copy you, so just talk me through the process, and I'll do exactly what you say—literally.

→ Was that harder than you thought it would be?

→ What did we learn about giving instructions?

→ What if you hadn't been able to watch me follow your instructions? What if this had taken place over the phone? How much more difficult would that be?

→ How can we use this to give better instructions?

SECTION 3

WHO: People-Driven Icebreakers

The roles people play in your life will help you pick the perfect icebreaker. Who are you speaking with? What kind of relationship do you have with them? Are you speaking with one or two people or to a group of 65? What kind of relationship do you want to have? This chapter offers icebreaker phrases tailored to people in different roles.

Perfect Phrases to Break the Ice When Interviewing Job Candidates

Good rapport helps you quickly recognize the potential of a job candidate. These phrases open the interview on a friendly note.

● Thanks for coming! Did anything interesting happen on the drive over? I get curious about what's happening outside these walls.

● We all have our favorite ways of getting directions. How did you get directions here?

- How did you hear about the opening? What made you decide to apply?

- Can I get you (soda, coffee, water)—a few stiff drinks? Kidding on the last one. There's nothing to be nervous about. I'm delighted you're here.

- I remember how nervous I was when I was on that side of the desk. I pictured it more as an interrogation than an interview, as if it didn't go both ways. I was really checking this company out as much as they were checking me out to see if it's a fit. So check us out all you want!

- One of the things I love about my job is that I get to meet with so many extraordinary people. I've had a chance to review your résumé, and I'm impressed by (example: your event management skill). I marvel that anyone can (example: handle that kind of detail).

- Before I start drilling you with questions, ☺ I'll tell you a little bit about the company and the position and give you a chance to ask me some questions.

- ❖ Before we start, I'll give you an overview of our new-hire selection process. Just an overview of the steps and stages.

- ❖ Before we do our presentation on the company and the position, let's go around the room and share how we first heard about the company and why we decided to come today. I'll go first. . . .

- ❖ I'd like for each of you to tell (me, us), in less than one minute, why you're the best candidate for this position.

- Let's start out with something fun! In a moment, I'll have you break into groups of three or four to discuss a solution to a problem. Pick one person to report on your solution.

You'll have (number) minutes to discuss the problem and come up with a solution. Here's the problem: (Explain industry-specific or generic problem. Example: How can you get customers to listen to your entire question before answering? Each group also could have a unique problem to discuss.)

→ I'd like a member of each team to describe how you reached the recommendations you did.

→ Great (creative, practical) ideas!

→ (To another interviewer in the room) Hey, were you taking notes? We might be able to use some of these ideas!

As you know, this job involves (example: sales). We'll give you up to three minutes to sell us, the whole group, on anything you want—a product, a service, or even a concept. Here's a wrinkle, though: you probably won't get to talk the whole three minutes. We'll stop you when we've heard enough of your pitch to get a feel for your skill. Don't feel bad if you don't get to finish your pitch. Just do your best right at the beginning. We will give you five minutes to think about what you want to sell and how you want to sell it. (Wait five minutes.)

→ Who wants to go first?

→ How did you pick that topic?

→ Why did you choose the approach you did?

Have you ever heard the phrase "do the worst first"? Well, that's what we're going to start with—what many people consider the worst or most nerve-wracking part of a group interview: the role play! Really, we just want you to have fun with it and get into the mindset of the (position). One person will play the (customer, client, patient), and the other person will play the (position). Here's the scenario: (industry-specific scenario; example: a tech support caller doesn't know how to reboot the computer). I'll take two volunteers to go first.

→ Excellent! Now, another pair.

→ What if the (customer, client, patient) is (slightly different scenario)?

→ Great. Now, the next group will role play the parts of (new scenario).

Perfect Phrases to Break the Ice with New Employees

It can be tough to be new, so choose icebreakers that both orient your new employees and put them at ease.

● Oh my gosh! You're our new (position). Welcome! I'm so glad you're here because (reason why they're welcome; example: we've been covering that position, and we really need your help.)

● You look a lot more relaxed than I did on my first day! I look forward to working with you.

● Ready to dive in? I have your first assignment letter ready for you with enough background information to get started. No need to delay as far as I'm concerned.

● I know that starting a new job can be overwhelming. So welcome, and know we're here to help! Trust me, we don't expect you to make it look easy in your first week! Or the second . . .

- I'm so glad you joined our team, and I'm here to answer your questions and give you a good footing for your first few days. I know I had plenty of questions when I started!

- Starting a new job is a little like going back to the first day of school, isn't it? At least it was for me. Don't worry—the gang—I mean, the employees—are great here.

- Hey! Welcome! You'll like working here because the team is (hardworking, dedicated, creative, willing to address conflict, able to give and accept feedback, customer focused). We're not perfect—don't get me wrong. But we're darn good at working things out when we need to.

- We look forward to adding your talents to the group! We need someone who knows how to (example: use the latest collaboration software).

- Hey! Welcome to the team! Let me tell you why you're going to love working here.

- Welcome. You've been assigned a buddy to help you get oriented. She'll be your go-to person. I'll introduce you.

- Let's take a tour of the (building, campus). I'll make sure to point out all the restrooms, watercoolers, and vending machines!

- I know you're probably experiencing information overload. Don't worry. We all felt that way at first.

- Ask me anything. Really! The only stupid question is the one you don't ask! Cliché—and true!

- I'll introduce you to some of the people you'll be working with. There's a test at the end to see if you remember all the names (☺). It's an open-book test, so don't panic!

- I'm (name) from (department). We don't talk among departments as much as I would like, so I figured I'd introduce myself early and invite you to let me know if there's anything I can do.

- You might feel like a rookie now, but in a few weeks people will be calling you the expert.

Perfect Phrases to Break the Ice with New Colleagues and Associates

When you're the new one, your peers might be so busy that they don't take the time to break the ice with you. Don't let that hold you back. Your first days aren't just about learning the technical aspects of the job. They're also about breaking in to the existing structure. Use some icebreakers of your own.

- Hi. I'm your new (position). I'd like to know what you liked most about the job my predecessor did so I can support you better.

- Hi! My name is (name), and my official job is to (function). I have a lot of unofficial skills too, so if you need help in different areas, let me know!

- I'm the new kid on the block. Got any tips for me?

- As your new (position), I consider you a customer, and I'm here to make your job easier. That's the plan, anyway, so let me know how I do!

- I've been here two whole days. How long did it take you to get into the flow when you started?

- I'm new. How did you learn the ropes when you first got here?

- I have a list of questions as long as my arm, but I don't know who to ask. Can you help me figure it out?

- I started here two days ago, and already I can tell you'd be a good person to know. I'm (name).

- Hi! I'm (name). What do you know now about working here that you wish you had known your first week here?

Perfect Phrases to Break the Ice with Supervisors and Leaders

Take the initiative to introduce yourself to a new manager or supervisor. While you might want to impress your manager or leader, you'll probably make a better impression if you speak to connect. In addition to generic icebreakers, the following can help you connect with those in charge.

- Congratulations on your new position! I can't wait to get started supporting you!

- I've heard great things about working with you. You know people say (genuine compliment you've heard), don't you?

- I'll learn your style over the days and weeks, but can you tell me anything to get me started learning about how to work with you?

- Glad to meet you! I'm new to you but not new to the industry. I look forward to supporting you and learning from you.

- I expect we'll be busy, so I'll give you the short version of my background.
- I'm excited to be a member of your team because (reason).
- Hi. I'm the new (position). I hear you're someone to know around here.
- My manager reports to you, and I wanted to meet you so I can support my manager better. I'm (name).
- Hi! I'm (name) and new here. I see my name here on the org chart and yours is upstream, so I figured we should meet.
- Glad to meet you. I'm (name). Please let me know how I can support you!

Perfect Phrases to Break the Ice with People Lower on Your Org Chart

Most generic icebreakers are fine for people lower on the org chart, because people are people wherever they are in the official hierarchy. We provide a few specific icebreakers here because employees are often intimidated by people higher up on the corporate ladder. Intimidation can keep employees from making suggestions, raising issues, and sharing their talents and skills beyond their job description. In addition to a generic icebreaker that implies you know we all put our pants on the same way, these specific phrases will open meaningful conversations.

- I'd like to get on a first-name basis with everyone. I'm (first name). Can I call you (first name)?

- I wanted to meet the person who (example: answers the phone) myself. I'm (name), and I appreciate the way (example: you greet people and make them feel so welcome).

- Hello. I'm (name), and I'm in charge of (area). I like to get out and see what's really happening on the front lines so I know how the decisions we make play out. Can I ask you some questions about the workflow since we (initiative)?

- It seems like everyone knows who I am around here, so I feel awkward not knowing your name. I'm (name). And you?

- It seems like everyone knows who you are around here, so I feel awkward about not knowing your name. I'm (name). What's your name?

- There's no way I could do the job you do. I know you know that, and I hope you know I know that too. I admire your expertise.

- I'm (name), and as your (leader, manager, etc.), it's my goal to set you up for success. Any tips on how I can do that better?

- I like to set people up for success. Is there anything I can do to make your job easier?

- You're doing a great job with (specific). Are there any skills that we don't use that you'd like to share with me?

Perfect Phrases to Break the Ice with Industry Professionals

How curious are you about other industry professionals? What can you learn from them? What kind of shared experiences do you have? Your genuine curiosity will guide the way you break the ice. These phrases will help.

- Does it seem to you that the industry is being turned on its head like it does to me? What changes have you noticed?

- I'm (name), and I'd love to share best practices with you if you're open to it.

- I get so focused on my own (practice, job) that I forget to wonder what other people are doing. How do you keep abreast of the industry?

- I love getting together with other (profession) because I learn so much. Would you like to mastermind with me sometime soon?

- Could I chat with you sometime to find out how business is in your industry?

- I bet you're tired of people offering to take you to coffee to "pick your brain." How about lunch? (☺)

- What are the new trends in your industry?

- How do you see your industry changing the most in the next few years?

- If you met someone just getting started in your industry, what would you tell that person?

- It's a big question, but what's the culture like in your industry? How would you describe it? Mine is (example: dynamic almost to the point of frenetic).

Perfect Phrases to Break the Ice with Service People

Without service people, organizations would fall apart. Sometimes the person to know is the one who can fix the air conditioner, unjam the copier, or keep you from using the sledgehammer on your computer. Don't wait until there's a crisis to make their acquaintance, though! Get some rapport going early, and often. And be sincere: people are really good about sensing "using" versus genuine interest and goodwill.

- Hi! I never see you without (tool), and without you, this place would fall apart. What's your name?

- Nothing like a good crisis to show us who the key players are around here.

- Boy, am I happy to see you! Our (problem) is bugging us to no end, and you're a real lifesaver. What's your name?

- I want to meet you before I need you, because when my (whatever they service) goes out, I get a little crazy!

- I already knew you were important, but today I'm finding out how important you really are.

- You come highly recommended by (referral source). How'd you get them thinking you walk on water?

- Is there anything you need from me to help you get the job done?

- I'm so glad we have a professional working on this!

- You make (their service) look really easy, but you're not fooling me! There's a reason I'm not in your profession. I'd last about a day!

- Hooray! You're here! I'll help by staying out of your way, unless there's something I can do for you.

Perfect Phrases to Break the Ice with Suppliers

The best vendor relationships are partnerships. You work together to make the relationship work for everyone. Cultivate vendors in the same way you cultivate your best client.

- Great to meet you! I like your (by-line, tagline, company slogan, e-mail signature code) (recite) because (reason). That made me want to call you.

- We're looking for new vendors to partner with for (product or service). I'm calling you because (reason).

- I've had some great relationships with suppliers in the past. May I tell you what my ideal supplier relationship is like? I'd love to hear what works for you too.

- I'd like to find out why your name keeps coming up when people talk about (product). What is it that makes you so popular?

- I need your help in evaluating (product or service). How does your (product or service) differ from other vendors' (products or services)?

- One thing that made your (example: ad, website) stand out was (distinguishing feature), and I had to call!

- Tell me about your (product, service, solution). What makes you stand out? What have you earned bragging rights for?

- What's your best-selling product?

- How would you describe your ideal customer?

- I've learned that a good vendor is just as important, probably more important than a good customer or client. How can I help you do what you need to do?

- I like working with vendors who see their role as educating and advising customers, not just selling products. I consider it a partnership, and I'd like us to work collaboratively like that. What do you think?

- If you can ensure that (example: this parts bin is never empty and every part you place in it meets our specifications), then we'll have a long and profitable relationship. How can I help you help me?

Perfect Phrases to Break the Ice with Potential Strategic Partners

Strategic partnerships are becoming increasingly important. Some potential partners might see you as competition until you address the mutual benefits of combining efforts. When you break the ice with someone who might make a good strategic partner, you can open with general shoptalk—or you could be completely upfront about your interest in exploring possibilities.

- I totally respect your work and see potential for a strategic partnership that could benefit both of us—and make great things happen.

- Hi, I'd like to explore the possibility of a strategic partnership in the area of (area). I'm a great collaborator and know the difference between being a strategic partner and being a parasite. Can we talk?

- Hi, (name). I love your work, and I suspect if we started talking for a few minutes we'd find ourselves talking for hours about our (businesses, work). Could we make that happen?

- I've always thought we should meet because (reason).

- As a (profession; example: engineer) I have some great ideas for (idea) but don't know a lot about (example: marketing). I would like to meet you for coffee to exchange ideas. My nickel. Possible?

- I see an opportunity to create (product or service) and don't have your (expertise; example: technical background in this industry) to know how viable it is. Could I get your opinion?

- I see a need for (product or service) and think there would be a huge market. It's not something I could do on my own, and I'm looking for someone who knows (area) like you do to collaborate with. Can we talk?

- I've admired your work from afar for years and want to get on your radar in case that admiration can grow into ways we can work together.

- You and I have such different (skill sets, businesses, backgrounds) that it might seem odd for us to consider combining forces. But I think the blending of our talents could open up a whole new world of business options for us both. Can we talk?

- You know what? I was thinking about you, and it occurred to me that there are opportunities for both of us to build credibility and leverage by working together.

- Your company is strong in (strength). My company is strong in (strength). Why don't we explore how we might make each other even stronger in the long run?

- I have some ideas how we might create a win-win situation by working together.

- I think we might make a good fit as potential strategic partners.

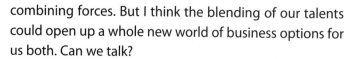

Perfect Phrases to Break the Ice with Potential Customers and Clients

Do you want to break the ice with someone who might be able to use your products or services? Don't dance around your purpose, but do resist the temptation to go right into selling—or even detailing what you do with potential customers of clients. Speak like a peer who has a clue of what it's like in their world and is open to knowing more.

- (Name) said we should talk. (She, He) told me you (business).

- I see you're in (industry). I work with a lot of industry professionals. What changes are you experiencing?

- I'd like to know more about your business. What are some projects you're working on these days?

- I read about your company. Aren't you working on (project)?

- I was on your website and noticed (observation).

- I'm working with other (example: CPA firms). I know they're struggling with (challenge). How are you handling that?

- I saw in the (example: *Denver Business Journal*) that you (example: have a new strategic initiative). What's it like implementing it?

- What was your career path to the position you have now? Where do you see yourself going next?

- I don't know if it's a fit, but I'd like to see if you might be able to use my services. Can I ask you a few questions about what you do, and see if there's a way I can help you?

Perfect Phrases to Break the Ice with Gatekeepers

You sometimes need to get past gatekeepers to reach decision makers. They can be your adversaries or your allies, depending on how you treat them.

- Hi, (name). I'm hoping you can help me. I need to (talk with, get some information to) (decision maker). What's the best way to do that?

- I hear you're the one to talk to about speaking with (name). Can I take just a few minutes of your time?

- Hi. I have some information for (name) that I'd like to make as relevant as possible. Can I ask you a couple of questions to make the best use of (decision maker's) time?

- Can you tell me the best way to reach (decision maker)? I know how busy (she, he) is and could use some tips.

- I have some ideas for (decision maker) and was hoping you'd be able to help me figure out how to present it in the best way to get (his, her) attention, interest, and understanding. I know you know (his, her) style better than anyone.

- If you were me, trying to reach (decision maker), how would you go about it?

Perfect Phrases to Break the Ice with Competitors

It's a wonderful thing to see competitors form partnerships. My videographer and other local videographers pass each other's names around and willingly refer business. Do they run the risk of losing a client to the other? Sure. And they are able to take better care of their customers that way, which ultimately benefits everyone. Here are some phrases to break the ice with a competitor who could become an ally.

- I've heard great things about your work! I'm in your industry. Let me know if there's anything I can do to support you!

- You and I are in the same business. I plan to refer well-suited customers to you and would appreciate it if you will do the same for me. Can we talk?

- We have some (customers, clients) in common. I've asked a few what they like about working with you, and several said (example: you listen really well to what they want).

- Hi! I'm your "collabortition." At least I like to see it that way. We're competing for (job, project, promotion), and if you get it, I'll support you any way I can.

- I was wondering what my competition looked like in this (service, project). I'm really glad to meet you. Let me know if I can be a resource to you.

- You and I are up for the same job in (area). I'm hoping I'll get the job, of course, but I wouldn't be embarrassed about losing to you.

- I'm (name), and I'm in the running for (project) too. I did a lot of research preparing for the application and interview, and if you get it, I'd love to share what I learned in case it's useful to you.

- I was hoping to get the (position, contract, etc.) for (area). I think you'll do a great job, and I want to let you know that if I can support you in your success, just ask.

- What do you think of competitors forming strategic alliances for mutual benefit? Is that something you've done? I ask because I'd like to check the possibility out with you.

- Our services overlap, but there are some areas where we don't compete. I'd like to know more about you and your business so I can refer jobs I can't handle to you. Open?

Perfect Phrases to Break the Ice with People from Other Cultures

Cultural difference can be awkward with lots of opportunities for foot-in-mouth syndrome. You need to watch out for stepping on cultural land mines, but even if you do, it can provide opportunities for great interaction.

- Aloha (bonjour, hola, saludo). (Hello in their native language, if you know it.)

- Do you mind my asking where you're from? I don't recognize your accent.
  - → I'm embarrassingly ignorant about your culture. When I show my ignorance, will you correct me?

- I'd like to know more about (culture, country). What is the most important (or most misunderstood) thing you think I should know?

- Hello! I don't know the polite form of greeting for your country. Can you help me with that?

- I'd love to see my culture through your eyes.
  - → What stands out as a big difference to you?
  - → What have you had to adapt to?
  - → What bothers you most when people from my culture work with people from your culture?

Perfect Phrases to Break the Ice with People with Disabilities

People with disabilities are people first. The same icebreakers you use with apparently nondisabled people work perfectly; comments on the weather, sports, the event you are attending, and so forth. Sometimes the disability presents itself as an issue that needs to be addressed or can even be a topic for connecting. Start out with a general icebreaker and then move to the specific situation.

- Hi. I'm (name). It looks like you could use some help. What can I do for you?

- Hi. I notice you seem to (identify the apparent disability). Is there anything I should know, do, or not do, to make you most comfortable?

- Hi. I'd be happy to (specific assistance; example: push your wheelchair, take you to a location, read the sign) if you would like me to.

- What a great (service animal). How long have you had him?
  → Is he always on duty?
  → Does everyone want to pet him?

- Hey there! This isn't the most accessible place, and if there is anything I can do to help you, I'd love to help out.

- We've tried hard to make this place accessible, but I know that nothing's perfect. Is there anything I can do to help you enjoy it fully? I'll certainly let management know of any improvements they can make.

- Hi. May I shake your hand? Is there anything I can see for you?

- I notice you have (disability; example: a visual impairment), and yet you get around really well. My (friend, parent, etc.) has that too. I'd love to pick your brain for tips for getting around your challenge I can share with (him, her).

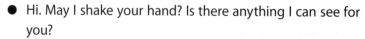

Perfect Phrases to Break the Ice When You Have a Disability

If you have a disability that affects your interactions with others, sometimes you'll want to explain what you need so that things go smoothly. In fact, your disability could even be an icebreaker. If you can include humor, all the better.

- Due to my (disability), I may need some help. I'll let you know in advance.

- Would you mind holding the door for me? I walk slowly.

- I used to pretend I don't have a disability, but I found it actually can make a great conversation opener. If you're at all curious, the topic is fair game as far as I'm concerned.

- I'm rehabbing my shoulders and can't reach those upper elevator buttons. I'm not tall enough to reach it with my nose, either. Would you please push (floor) for me?

- I don't hear very well, and your voice is in the worst range for me. Would you please rephrase what you just said? And if you could try to sound a little more like (example: John Wayne) that would be even better.

- I don't hear very well. Could you face me when you speak?
- I hear better on my left (right) side. Could you talk on that side?
- My glasses don't give me good vision; they just let me avoid walking into doors—most of the time. Let me know if you see an errant doorway looking to attack me!

Perfect Phrases to Break the Ice with People Who Can Help You Succeed

There are people you will want to meet mainly because of what they can do for you. People in power and with resources understand that, so you're better off not pretending you're calling the CEO's assistant because of her dazzling personality when you're really calling to get on the CEO's calendar. That doesn't mean that you should ignore the personal aspect, however. Be straightforward and yet graceful.

- Hi! I've been told you're the go-to person for (help). They tell me you're the one to know. We haven't met, and I'd like to change that.
- People say you're the one to know for people who want to (what you want help with). I'm sure you get requests all the time. How do you like people to approach you about it?
- I've wanted to get to know you for a long time, and it's a bit awkward to be calling you now, because I have a favor to ask. Do you have a minute?

● Hi. I'm (name, title if relevant). I am in awe of your (accomplishment). I know that your time is valuable, and I'd like very much to learn from you. Would you have any time to teach me (something specific), or could you suggest someone else I could learn from?

● I'm where you might have been years ago in your career. Could I ask you a few questions?

● I've admired what you've accomplished. I suspect a few minutes of your time could save me a lot of fumbling around. Might you help me out?

● I heard you were interested in (topic, project, charity, etc.), and I am working on a project that I think you'd like to see succeed. Can we talk?

● Your name comes up a lot as someone who could help me with (project). When (name) suggested we talk, I knew it was time for me to pick up the phone.

● I'm working on something important, and I need your help. Could you spare a few minutes to talk about it?

SECTION 4

WHAT: Topic-Driven Icebreakers

Common topics for breaking the ice may seem cliché, but they've become cliché only because the topics intimately affect us. With a little creativity, finesse, and alignment with purpose, cliché topics can serve your ice-breaking mission well.

Perfect Phrases to Break the Ice by Talking about Weather

Why is weather a common topic for breaking ice? Because it's a shared experience that affects us all. Weather affects us in interesting ways. It changes our plans, and it changes our moods. We all have extreme weather stories. No one goes untouched by the weather, and how we respond to it gives clues to who we are.

- I was reading about the (tornados in the Midwest, hurricanes on the Gulf Coast, earthquakes on the West Coast), and my heart went out to those people. Have you ever been through anything like that?

- This downpour is captivating, isn't it! Yes! Pun intended!
- Did you come prepared for this weather?
- Were they predicting this?
- I love this kind of weather—at least, when I don't have to go anywhere. How about you?
- The weather forecast for the weekend is (sunny, rainy, snow). Do you have plans to be outside?
- When the weather is like this, it makes me wonder about living here! What places do you think have ideal weather?
- Remind me why I live in this state! I love it, but I wonder when the weather gets like this.
- Well, at least we don't live in (Antarctica, Death Valley). What's the (coldest, hottest) day you can remember?
- How does the weather affect your business? Or does it?
- What's the craziest weather you've ever been in?
- Hey, crazy weather we've been having.
  - → Does weather like this keep you indoors?
  - → How do you entertain yourself in this kind of weather?
  - → How do you enjoy this kind of weather?
  - → I (am, am not) a (hot, cold) weather person. Are you?

Perfect Phrases to Break the Ice by Talking about Recreation and Hobbies

Get people talking about their recreation and hobbies, and you've tapped into their passion. Tell them a bit about your recreation and hobbies and you've given them insight into your nature. It helps if you can segue gracefully from the current activity to the hobby, but many people jump through the smallest of openings to talk about things they love.

- Hi! I'm a (profession) by day and a (hobby) by night. You?
- This meeting is almost as fun as (your hobby). What do you do for fun?
- On a day like today, I'd almost like to play hooky and (hobby). What would you be doing if you weren't here?
- I see from your (clue, such as hat, notebook, bumper sticker) that you (hobby). What can you tell someone who knows little about it but is curious?
- My game is golf. What's yours?
- I work mostly to support my (hobby) habit. Aside from work, how do you like to spend your time?
- I'm looking to find someone who (hobby) to learn more about it. Are you into it?

Perfect Phrases to Break the Ice by Talking about Clothes

In theory, clothes are a personal topic and therefore off limits for breaking the ice in business settings. In practice, they can get a great conversation going fast. It's more common for women to admire, inquire, and share shopping tips about clothes than men, but the guys have been known to break the ice effectively through the clothing conversation as well. Just avoid flirting. And be sensitive to the purpose and tone of the meeting. I've led the last activity in this section very successfully in women's image classes but wouldn't even imagine doing it at a process improvement meeting.

Consider this fun tip: you can wear your own icebreaker— some kind of conversation piece that always gets comments. Here are some phrases for you.

- I see you got the same memo I did about dressing for this event! Love those colors!

- I want to be there when you clean out your closets! Love your style!

- I just saw Clinton Kelly's "What Not to Wear" show. He'd have no place to start with you. Great style!

- Is that (example: Chicos)? I love their jackets.

- I'm so glad I'm not the only one who's (example: wearing flats).

- I've been looking for a (purse, tie, shoes, etc.) just like that! Where did you get it?

- I see you have a (name of organization) pin. Have you been a member long?

- I keep forgetting what the ribbon colors mean. What does the color of your pin mean?
  → Why do you wear it?

- Comfortable shoes! I'm so glad someone else is wearing them too!

- I wish I'd thought to wear (example: a sweater) today. You thought ahead!

● That's an unusual (tie, pin, necklace). What's the story behind it?

🎬 Let's break into groups. Now, we'll each tell a story about something we're wearing. For example, I got this necklace from my mother's estate. She had lots of fun jewelry.

→ Did any of you find there's more to what you're wearing than you had imagined?

→ Was it hard to think of a story about something that you were wearing?

→ When someone else told a story, did you find that his or her story reminded you of a story?

→ Let's hear some of your stories. But I want you to share someone else's story, not your own!

Perfect Phrases to Break the Ice by Talking about Professional Sports

People take their teams very seriously. If you don't get elated when your team wins and depressed when your team loses, you might miss the value of sports as an ice-breaking opportunity. These phrases will help you use sports to get a conversation going.

● Did you (see, hear, read) the news today? How about them (Cubs)?

● I'm a little tired today because I stayed up watching the Olympics. Do you watch them?

● I like to think of myself as the Babe Ruth of (profession; example: business book writing), and in some ways I am.

He hit a lot of homers, and he also struck out quite a bit. Who do you compare yourself to?

● I read that Michael Jordan missed more than 9,000 shots in his career and lost almost 300 games. He was a loser, huh? Kidding!

❖ Let's go around the room and talk about great sports figures and what makes them so good.

🎬 Let's talk sports teams for a minute. Who has a sport they follow?

→ Describe how the team works together for success.
→ Can you tell me how great coaches help (team) succeed?
→ What inspires you about the game?
→ What does it mean to be a team player in that sport?
→ What famous athletes do you know about who aren't the best team players?

🎬 Let's start this meeting off with a shout-out to our favorite teams. And limit your objections to supporters of opposing teams to dirty looks, OK? I'll start. Go (example: Broncos)!

Perfect Phrases to Break the Ice by Talking about Family

Most people's hearts are with their families. Conversations and references to family are a good way to forge a bond. But before you trot out the old familiar "do you have any kids?" question, make sure you care enough to listen to the answer and to build on a yes or no. It's better not to go there if you're just "making conversation."

- Do you get to spend enough time with your family?

- I was thinking about where to try out all the new skills we're learning, and I got it! Family! After all, they never criticize. Right? Oh, wait . . .

- I plan to try out some of the ideas I'm learning on my kids. They can't leave—they don't have any money. How are you going to try out what you're learning?

- I love these conferences, but I feel so guilty being here at (place) without my kids. They'd just love the (place or event). Who are you missing?

- I know I'm traveling too much because I've run out of "thinking about you" gift ideas. What do you plan to get your family members? I could use some ideas.

- Are you going to be buying an "I missed you" gift at the airport, too?

- I'm looking for some fun things to do in the area with my family. What are some things your family likes to do?

- How do you stay connected with your family when you travel? I'm thinking we might start using Skype or FaceTime.

- Have you ever worked somewhere that felt like family? Well . . . maybe minus the fighting?

- Sometimes my kids tell me to "get a life." I tell them I have a life. I like working and watching the rain fall. How about you?

- If you were going to explain (this idea, our business, etc.) to your family, how would you do it?

Perfect Phrases to Break the Ice by Talking about Current Events

Politics are touchy, but most of us are moved when we hear about a natural disaster or an act of heroism. I like to break the ice with strangers and people I don't know well by talking about current events in the same way I would mention a current event that moves me with someone I know.

- I had a hard time breaking myself away from the news today to get here on time. Have you been watching what's going on with (topic)?

- Oh my gosh! Did you read about (news you find inspiring, such as new uses for waste). What's the headline in your newspaper today?

- I read some good news today. I was so surprised I forgot what it was!

- Have you ever wondered why so much of the news is negative? Sometimes it seems like the only positive news is about weather and sports, and even that doesn't happen much! What good news have you heard lately?

- How do you get most of your news? Newspapers, TV, or online?

- ❖ Let's open by talking about recent events (example: a nuclear disaster) and how they affect our company.

- 🎬 We're going to play a current events question-and-answer game. We'll form teams.
  - → What part of the United States is experiencing drought right now?

→ How did the stock market do last week?
→ Is Congress in session right now?
→ How'd we do?

Perfect Phrases to Break the Ice by Talking about Movies and Entertainment

I overheard some people I didn't know discuss a television show that I wouldn't care to watch once, let alone follow. It didn't matter that I thought it was a pretty dumb show. It helped two strangers break the ice by talking about entertainment. You might not want to build an entire relationship around "The Biggest Loser," but don't overlook the opportunity to break the ice by talking about movies and entertainment.

● I'm imagining how to turn this situation into a sitcom. I might actually watch it! How about you?

● I thought twice about attending this conference when I realized it conflicted with the release of (movie). Are you into the series?

● I like to keep up with the latest in entertainment, but I just can't get into vampires. Do you have the same challenge, or are you someone who can explain the appeal to me?

● Streaming Netflix, cable, or dish? What's your home entertainment choice?

▪ Think of your favorite movie or television show. Write the name down.

→ Now, let's go around the room and share our choices. After each title, we'll come up with three ways that show relates to (example: our meeting purpose).

→ Now, let's go around the room and share our choices. After each title, we'll come up with three things we can learn from the show or movie that will help us succeed as a team.

🎬 Think about a hero from one of your favorite stories or movies. Got it? Write down the hero's name.

→ Now, let's go around the room and share our hero and how that hero would act in this situation.

→ Notice any recurring themes?

→ How many heroes were perfect?

→ What do you think it would take to be a hero in this situation?

→ Can there be a team of heroes?

Perfect Phrases to Break the Ice by Talking about Books

Books take us on journeys and adventures. If you share an interest in a certain book with someone, you might find yourself to be traveling mates. If you invite someone to share about a book you haven't read, that person can take you on a journey too. Either way, it's a great way to break the ice. Some phrases:

● I'm going to use an old icebreaker to see if I can start a conversation with you. Read any good books lately?

● I'm looking for a good (business book, novel) to read on my next trip. Any recommendations?

● I'm looking for someone else who's read (book title) to see if they liked it. Might that someone be you? Have you read it?

- That looks like a good book! Tell me about it.
  - → What strikes you most about it?
  - → Would you recommend it?
- I'm reading (title) and looking for someone else who's read it. Have you?
- I'd like to read a book that doesn't have (explosions, airplanes, vampires) on the cover. Got any suggestions?

🎬 Think of a book or magazine or even an interesting blog that you've read in the past couple of weeks.
  - → Now, pair up and share why you read it and what you thought about it. I'll give you about five minutes to talk.
  - → What did you learn about the book or magazine?
  - → What did you learn about your partner?

Perfect Phrases to Break the Ice by Talking about Technology

Since we tend to wear our technology these days, it presents a great opportunity for us to break the ice—and even learn a few things. True techies don't need anyone to give them icebreaker phrases to start conversations; they're naturally guided by their curiosity. But in case you haven't figured out how to break the ice with talk about the latest app or device, here are some phrases to get you started.

- I like asking everyone I see with a smartphone what their favorite app is. What's yours?

- I think we can all agree that having cell phone ringers off is a good idea. But what about using cell phones, laptops, or other personal technology during a face-to-face meeting? Good? Bad?

- Why did you choose (example: an Android instead of an iPhone)?

- I notice that you have an (iPhone, Blackberry, HTC). How do you like it?

- I love my Crackberry! I mean Blackberry! Is there some technology you can't live without?

- Kindle or Nook? I hear good things about both.

- I'm in the market for a new netbook, tablet, or laptop. Do you have any suggestions?

- I'm trying to figure out the best way to (keep track of contacts, schedule meetings, etc.). What works for you?

❖ Let's go around the room and share our favorite apps and why we like them.

🎬 Let's do a technology check-in before we proceed.
   → We'll start with what's working.
   → Great. Now, what's not working so well? Who has been tempted to reach for the sledgehammer?
   → Who needs help with some particular technology they're using?
   → Who wants permission to geek out on us here and tell us what we're not doing with our technology that we could be?

Perfect Phrases to Break the Ice by Talking about Immediately Shared Experiences

Most of the icebreakers in this book springboard off immediately shared experiences. This section gives you a few all-purpose shared-experience icebreakers. Note: People often bond by complaining together. That's a potentially effective icebreaker, but generally we recommend lightening complaints with playful humor or saying something more constructive.

- Did anyone else figure they got their exercise for a week just walking from the hotel to the conference room? I hope we didn't lose anyone in transit.

- Well, *that* was different. What do you think of (something that just happened)?
    - ➜ By the way, in my world, different isn't wrong by default.

- I didn't mind getting wet coming here today. We needed the rain. How about you?

- Did you notice how long the line was for the session on (topic)? I wonder why it's so popular?

- Now I know why it's called the Dallas–Fort Worth Airport. You have to walk from Dallas to Fort Worth to get to your gate!

- I'm going to have to run laps around the hotel to work off all this food they've been serving us!

- First, I'd like all of us to pick up our pens and look at our notes.
    - ➜ Next, write down anything you noticed in this room that is different from before. No peeking!

→ Now, let's share our observations.

→ Who realized you missed some really obvious changes?

→ What does that tell you about your observations?

→ Can you tell me what you think the point of this activity is or could be?

→ What other points could this activity make?

🎬 (For groups of four to six people. Larger groups can be divided.) We are going to play a game called "Same and Different." First, break up into groups of about five people.

→ Now, each group needs a piece of paper and a pen.

→ Select one person in your group to be the note taker, and make a list of how you all are similar. Now, I don't want the obvious stuff like "we all have eyes." Dig a little deeper than that. I'll give you five minutes.

→ Now I'll give you another five minutes to make a list of how you're all different. I want lists of qualities that only one person in your group has. Again, try to dig deeper than the obvious. Anyone need more paper?

→ Raise your hand if your group's list of "same" is longer than your list of "different."

→ Let's hear about some of your unique qualities.

Perfect Phrases to Break the Ice by Talking about Success

Many people focus too much on the negative. Talking about wins and success not only breaks the ice, but it also reminds people of their strengths. Here are some phrases.

● I heard you did a great job handling (project). Tell me about it!

● If you were asked for the recipe for success soup, what would be in it?

● I'm a student of what works. How have you made meetings like this work?

● I know we're all here to become more successful, and I wonder, how do you define success?

● I notice this group seems to define success as (example: making a lot of money, fame). I'm curious, how do you define it?

🎬 Let's go around the room and fill in the blank.
→ The surprising thing about success is _____ _____.
→ This project will be successful if _____.
→ One thing I learned from past success that will help us here is _____.

🎬 Let's talk about success, what it is and how our perceptions of it have changed over the years.
→ When you were in elementary school, how did you define success?
→ When you left school, how did you define success?
→ How do you define success today?
→ How have our perceptions changed?
→ How can we define success for today's meeting?

🎬 We're going to make success fortunes for each other. Take the card in front of you.
→ Now write a fortune for someone. For example, "You will make a point that will change how everyone thinks

about something today." Or, "You will learn something that will help you succeed." Or, "You will get a burning question answered."

→ If you want, make your fortune dependent on how the person participates. For example, "You will leave this meeting transformed if you admit where you're confused about something." Or, "You'll have a great idea during this meeting if you keep your texting to the topic of this meeting."

→ You can make fortunes about career, job, or task success, such as, "You will exceed expectations in this project." Or, "You will learn a new skill that will move your career forward exponentially."

→ Now I'll collect the fortunes, shuffle, and let you pick one.

→ (Name), what is your fortune? How do you relate to it? Is there anything you can do to help make that happen?

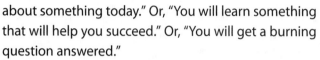

Perfect Phrases to Break the Ice by Talking about Possibilities

We all have an inner idealist who can imagine a perfect world that transcends current reality. We also have a less idealized vision of actual possibilities that can inspire us. Dreaming together is a great way to connect. Here are some phrases.

● What excites you about this (project, conference, meeting)?

❖ In the best of all possible worlds—if everything happened just the way we wanted it to—what would happen?

❖ Imagine we're looking back at this project, pleased and surprised by all we accomplished. What are we so happy about?

🎬 I used to be a perfectionist, but now I just like to imagine perfection as a guiding image.

→ Let's go around the room and imagine a vision of perfection for this project.

→ What keeps us from being there already?

→ What could we change or do that might remove that obstacle?

🎬 In my perfect world, meetings run like this: (your vision; example: we start on time, stick to the agenda, etc.). How about in yours?

→ Where do our visions compete?

→ Where are our visions aligned?

→ What can we do to move toward our perfect worlds?

🎬 Let's tell a tall tale about our (team, company, organization). We'll tell it like we've arrived at perfection. I'll start. In our organization, every moment of every day is spent on the important activities. There is never any need for firefighting. OK, you're next. Tell us something else about how perfect we are.

→ How did it feel to describe a vision of perfection?

→ Were any of us tempted to become sarcastic?

→ Can we talk about perfection without putting ourselves down for being human?

→ How does imagining perfection motivate or demotivate you?

Perfect Phrases to Break the Ice by Talking about Mistakes and Learning Experiences

It's great when people are willing to talk about mistakes and things they've done that haven't gone as well as they had hoped. It's not only better but also easier to get them to talk about the lessons they've learned from the past. Here are some conversation starters for you.

- I'm here because I tried to (example: build a website on my own) and failed. What inspired you to come?

- I found I learn more from my mistakes than from my successes. One lesson I've learned is (lesson). What's a lesson you've learned from your mistakes?

- Over the years, I've learned to fall pretty well. That makes me more willing to take risks. What have you learned about falling down and picking yourself back up?

- My (husband, wife) complimented me on my ability to fall down well when we cross-country ski. It really was a compliment! Let's go around the room and share examples about how learning to fall well was a key to success.
  - → Who here never thought about falling well or failing gracefully as a success skill before?

- This is an exercise to practice being more open to messing up. Let's count off. Remember your number. I'll start. One. (Etc.) Got your number?
  - → Number one is the beginning of the line. Number (highest number) is the end. So I'm number one, and that means I'm first.

→ I'm going to call out a number. If it's your number, respond by calling out someone else's number. If someone calls out your number, and you don't respond, you go to the number one position of the line behind me. The person who messes up will become number one. Every time someone becomes the new number one, everyone else's number goes up by one.

→ If you blow it, instead of grimacing, celebrate. Wave your hand in the air and say "Woohoo!" We'll all applaud, and then you'll call out a number.

→ How did it feel to miss your cue?

→ How did it feel to see other people miss theirs?

→ Did the applause take the sting out of missing?

→ How can we use this to get over our mistake phobia in life?

→ Who learned from missing and developed a system to keep on top of the game?

→ What do you think the point of this activity is?

Perfect Phrases to Break the Ice by Talking about Desired Outcomes

Where are you now? And where do you want to be? Talking about desired outcomes not only breaks the ice; it moves the conversation forward. Here are some icebreakers for you.

● We have (example: half an hour). I want to be sure you leave with what you need. What would you like to accomplish?

● What are you hoping to get out of this (conference, class, meeting)?

- ● What can I do for you? What would you like to have happen?

- ❖ Let's picture ourselves at the end of this (meeting, discussion) feeling good about the outcome. What are we feeling good about?

- ❖ I would love for us to walk out of this room having achieved (specific outcome; example: agreement). What would you love us to achieve?

- ❖ In a perfect world, what would the ideal outcome be?

- ❖ By the end of this (meeting, project), this is where I would like us to be.

- 🎬 This is where we are now. (Summarize.) This is where we're going. (Summarize.) The next big question is, how will we get there?
  - → What do you see as the first step?
  - → How will we determine the second one?

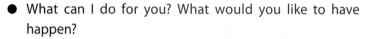

Perfect Phrases to Break the Ice by Talking about Best Practices

What is that person you just met—or the person you've known forever, but not as well as you might like—doing that you could learn from? What best practice do you have that could rock someone else's world? Some phrases:

- ● This is a great conference, but I haven't heard anyone mention the one thing that is my all-time favorite best practice. Did you know that (practice; example: you can set mail rules to sort your inbox)?

- You know, I realized you and I could be great resources for each other. I've got a few best practices I'd like to share. How about you?

- (Name) suggested (example: getting a daily meeting with your manager) as a best practice, but I just haven't been able to get it to work because (reason; example: we come in at different times). What am I overlooking?

- I look at everyone I meet as a teacher. And I hope that others see me the same way. Of course, sometimes I'm just a warning of what not to do. ☺ But I've learned a few best practices I'd love to share. How about you?

❖ Let's share best practices for saving time.

❖ Who has a best practice for remembering things?

❖ Does anyone have a best practice for remembering what you've forgotten?

🎬 Let's open by sharing best practices. Turn to your neighbor, and share one thing you do that works really well for you. It could be here at work, at home, with a hobby—anything.
    → Who heard a best practice that will be useful to them?
    → What was it?

🎬 How do you start with a jigsaw puzzle? Let's go around the room.
    → Who learned an approach that seems useful?
    → How could you apply that to projects at work?

Perfect Phrases to Break the Ice by Talking about Personality and Communication Styles

Communication and personality styles are the new astrology. People like talking about them. There are many style assessments to draw from. I provide a communication inventory at www.speakstrong.com/inventory that describes four styles: Reflective, Directive, Likable, and Visionary. While I caution against sounding like you're trying to put someone you've just met in a box, styles can be a great conversation starter.

● Have you taken any tests to find out your style? Personality, work, or communication? Which ones do you like?

● I've done the colors and the Strength Finder and Myers-Briggs and all kinds of style tests, and I still don't know how to talk to my kids. How about you?

❖ (Talk about yourself; example: As a Reflective I tend to like to wait for other people to initiate a conversation, but today I'll take the lead.)

🎬 Raise your right hand if you're more task-oriented than people-oriented.

→ Now raise your left hand if you move at a swifter pace—a faster clip than most.

→ If you have both hands up, your communication style is Directive. If you have just your right hand up, your communication style is Likable. If you have only your left hand up, you're more of a Visionary. If you don't have any hands up, you're pretty much a Reflective.

→ Let's start with the Directives and talk about how we like people to communicate with us.

🎬 Let's go around the room and share communication styles and how they affect how we act at meetings.
  → What do you want people with different styles to know about yours?
  → How have you adapted your style to other people?

🎬 Let's talk about play.
  → Define play. What is it? What isn't it? What are the features of play? I'll list what you tell me.
  → What features of play apply to work? How?
  → Are there ways we make our work harder than it needs to be?
  → How can we effectively add playfulness to our work?
  → How does our (communication, personality) style affect our definitions of play?

Perfect Phrases to Break the Ice by Talking about Personal Traits

Like communication styles, personal traits can provide material for a great icebreaker. We're all a little quirky, and this can be a way to share our humanity.

- I really like getting to know new people. How about you?
- I find it difficult to sit still for this long. Do you?
- I'd almost rather skip vacation than deal with the built-up e-mail when I get home! How about you?
- Some people like to think before they speak, and others speak in order to think. Which one are you?

I'd like the people at each table to find three traits you have in common.

→ What are they?

→ Now, break into pairs. Your goal is to find one unique trait or experience you have in common.

→ What did you uncover?

→ What was different about sharing in pairs over sharing in a group?

→ Who feels closer to their partner knowing that you share that trait?

Perfect Phrases to Break the Ice by Talking about What We're Proud Of

Most of us have been taught to be modest. Permission to brag about our accomplishments and the things we're proud of can be very freeing. Some phrases:

● OK, so what would you like to brag about? I worked hard to get here! How about you?

● How did you get where you are in the industry?

● Were you born with the ability to (skill) or is it something you developed?

● You're going through a major transition and while there are some balls that have been dropped in the process, I think it's pretty heroic to do what you're doing. So I have a question for you. Are there things you'd like to be acknowledged for? Ways you're standing up where you used to crumble; ways you're being graceful where you haven't always been; and ways you know you're being courageous that might not be apparent with all the fires you're fighting?

❖ Let's start this meeting by bragging about something we achieved in the last week. Or whenever. Something we deserve a pat on the back for.

❖ Let's review our team successes and applaud each one.

❖ Let's go around the circle and describe our best qualities in one or two words. Something we're proud of. I'll start. (Example: I'm pretty flexible. I can roll with the punches and keep moving toward getting things done.) Next?

🎬 Let's each share a winning moment in our careers.

→ How similar or different were our ideas of winning?

→ How many of us felt a need to qualify our wins by pointing out where others helped, how we weren't perfect, and that kind of thing?

🎬 What does our (team, organization) do really, really well? It doesn't need to be a huge deal—it could be little things. Write your ideas, and we'll go around and share them.

→ How did our jobs affect what we chose?

→ Is there a theme?

→ How does it influence you to discuss our strengths?

→ Can you talk about strengths without wanting to immediately qualify them?

Perfect Phrases to Break the Ice by Talking about Holidays

Although different cultures have different holidays, there is a universal quality to them, and many holidays are based on seasons that we all share. These phrases will help you start a conversation by talking about the holidays.

- How do you celebrate the holidays?
- Do you do anything unusual to celebrate the holidays?
- Are you ready for the holidays?
- I can't keep up with all the holidays anymore. How about you?
- One thing I love about the holidays is (example: how they mark the changing seasons). How about you?
- What's your favorite holiday?
  - → What makes it special for you?
  - → How long have you celebrated it?
- I loved the holidays as a kid! What's your favorite (memory, holiday tradition) from when you were a kid?
- What is the most interesting (holiday) tradition you saw or know of?

 Take a minute to write down two things you like about the holiday season—no matter what you do or don't celebrate.
  - → Let's share our lists.
  - → How do the holidays affect our work together?
  - → How can we celebrate holidays inclusively, so no one feels as if they're supposed to celebrate the way we do or that we don't honor how they celebrate?

Perfect Phrases to Break the Ice by Talking about Preferences and Peeves

People love talking about their pet peeves. We caution about coming across as negative, but if you avoid a downward spiral, you can use pet peeves to start conversations. You also can move the discussion forward by being lighthearted and transforming a peeve conversation into a conversation about preferences.

● Did you notice they put the toilet paper on the *wrong* way here? Makes me wonder about them! (You do know I'm kidding, right?)

● Is it me, or is (peeve) just plain *wrong*?

🎬 Let's open the discussion with our meeting pet peeves—and preferences. For example, it bugs me when someone texts during a meeting. I prefer the focus stay in the room. How about you? Please list three pet peeves that you have at work or at home.

→ Now, let's go around the room and share a story about a positive way you handled a situation when someone's behavior peeved you.

→ Why are we all so quiet? ☺

→ OK, I'll start with mine. When (example: checkout people put the bills in my hand first and the change on top of that), it's one of my biggest pet peeves. In the grand scheme of things, I know it's not that big a deal. I've learned (to tell when that's about to happen and start to put the bills away before they can pile the change on top).

Perfect Phrases to Break the Ice by Talking about Attitudes

If you open conversations, meetings, and presentations in ways that make people conscious of their attitudes, they are far more likely to be constructive in their dialogue and interactions. These ice-breaking phrases will help.

- Attitudes are contagious, and it looks like you have one I'd like to catch.

- I could use an attitude adjustment about this meeting. I think I'm getting in my own way here. Any ideas or tips on how you keep yours elevated?

- Are you as positive as you appear? I'd like to know your secret.

- Some coach said winning isn't everything, it's the only thing. I'm inclined to say that same thing about attitude. How do you keep yours positive?

 Let's play with attitudes. First, let's make a list of things we'd like to do someday. Get a motorcycle, build a dream house—whatever your wish list suggests.

- → Now we'll all review these ideas like Eeyore, the donkey from *Winnie the Pooh*. We'll all be doom and gloom. Our job is to negate everything. Find the fly in every ointment, the reason not to do things. We'll start with the first idea and have some target practice. Say things like "too expensive" or "too dangerous." That kind of thing.

- → How did the attitude affect the discussion? How might it affect the chances of realizing that dream?

➔ Now we'll review the same dreams as hopeless optimists. We'll minimize or ignore any pitfalls, potential obstacles, and so forth, and blindly encourage each other.

➔ How did the optimistic attitude affect the discussion?

➔ Now let's be realistically encouraging. We'll reflect on the wishes by talking about what steps would move the dreamer toward the goal and how he or she might make a fondest wish happen.

➔ How did the realistic encouragement affect the discussion?

➔ If you were seriously considering pursuing that wish, what kind of attitude would be most helpful in getting you there?

🎬 Stand up and pair off. Partner A is the taller one.

➔ Raise your hands, and place your palm against your partner's. Partner A, push.

➔ Partner B, what did you do when your partner pushed on you? Pushed back!

➔ How does an aggressive, pushy attitude open a conversation? What response does that inspire?

➔ How could we open in a more productive way?

➔ When someone pushes on us, what options do we have besides pushing back?

🎬 We're going to do an attitude adjustment exercise. We'll start with listing some emotions and qualities associated with really bad attitudes. Fill in this sentence: I know I need an attitude adjustment when I feel _____. Note: you don't get to use the words "feel like." We're going for attitudes here, such as mad, sad, and scared. Frustrated, helpless, victimized, and powerless. Got it? Go!

→ Every emotion exists for a reason. It's a signal. For example, my anger tells me things aren't the way I want them. It's a signal to take some action to set a boundary or make a change. Let's go through the list and see what our emotions are signaling.

→ Great. Now let's take each emotion and decide what the goal of an attitude adjustment would be. For example, my anger is a signal I want to flip into determination. That will be more likely to get me a good outcome. My frustration is a signal to flip into fascination. That will help me learn what I need to in order to resolve what's frustrating me. Got it? Let's go through the list.

→ Now find a partner. Partner A is the one with the larger shoe size. OK, A, go through the list and tell your partner that he or she seems to have the emotion on the left—the bad attitude emotion. For example, say to Partner B, "You seem (emotion; example: hostile)" using the first bad attitude emotion on the list. Partner B, respond by saying, "Close. Actually I'm (emotion; example: feisty)," using one of the target emotions on the list.

→ If the target emotion feels unobtainable to you, keep trying other ones until you find a constructive emotion you believe you can at least move into.

→ How did it feel to claim a nobler version of each emotion?

→ How could this affect your ability to successfully handle challenging situations?

🎬 Stand up and face your partner. Partner A, you will make a suggestion to Partner B about vacations, recreation, possible projects, and so on. For example, you could say,

"Partner B, it would be great if you posted the procedures you've developed to the intranet." Partner B, you will respond with the words "Yes, but," and follow with all the reasons that couldn't happen. For example, "Yes, but that would take a long time." Ready? Go!

→ Now, A, same thing, only B will respond with "Yes, and." Follow your "and" with an alternative, such as, "Yes, and I could send them to the web developer to post." Ready? Go!

→ How did you feel when your partner kept "yes-but-ing" you?

→ Who came up with some great plans?

→ How can we use this in discussions and arguments?

→ What is the difference in attitude between the two terms?

Perfect Phrases to Break the Ice by Talking about Words

Of course, Diane and I are word people. That's a given, considering our professions. Many people share our love for words, and words are a great way to break the ice. Here are a few icebreakers that talk about words.

● "Ello-hay!" That's Pig Latin for "Hello!" Do you know other ways to say "Hello?"

● Have you ever met someone who thinks out loud? Sometimes I don't know what words to use until I say them. Are you like that? Or do you think out your words first?

- I've heard it said that a picture is worth a thousand words. What does that mean for video?

- Remember that childhood rhyme, "Sticks and stones may break my bones, but words will never hurt me"? Is that true for you?

- Are you ever at a loss for words? Like I am right now?

- Do you remember playing word association games as a kid? I say a word, and then you say the first word that comes to your mind? For example, I say "black" and you say "white." Let's go back and forth and see what comes up!

🎬 Who knows what a sniglet is?

→ A sniglet is a coined word for something without a specific name. Or it's something that should be in the dictionary but isn't. Words like "anniversorry," the act of buying presents to make up for a forgotten anniversary. Make sense?

→ We're going to break into groups and invent our own sniglets. Let's think of everyday things that happen that we can't just use one word for. For example, how about people who spend hours on Facebook every day? "Facebookaholics"?

→ What did the teams come up with?

🎬 I have a few words embedded into today's (meeting, presentation). Make a note each time you hear these words. There will be a prize for the person who catches them most.

→ Derivatives count. For example: *Polemic* and *assiduous* are today's words and *polemics* and *assiduously* count.

→ Note: I will try to trick you, so be *assiduous*, even when my *polemics* make it hard. And if you're at six now, you've got the idea.

Perfect Phrases to Break the Ice by Talking about Responsibility and Accountability

Does opening with the topic of responsibility and accountability sound like guaranteed buzz kill? Well, I wouldn't use it at a cocktail party, but in some environments it can actually get genuine, interesting, and important conversations started.

- I heard that you're the person to talk to if I need someone I can count on. Is that true?

- This project isn't for the faint of heart. It's for people with a high level of integrity who understand what responsibility and accountability mean. We need to know we have each other's backs. Are we there? Can I count on you to do what you say, every time?

❖ Our first commitment needs to be to the goal of (example: launching the project on time). Our commitment to each other is also a commitment to that goal. If we let our team members slack, we're not supporting them; we're enabling them.

❖ I'm the facilitator here, but I want and need each one of you to make the meeting your own and contribute to the success as if it were yours.

❖ This will be a great ride—but with a destination. We need to keep our commitment to outcome front and center. Let's go around the room and talk about what that means.

🎬 Describe a time when you worked on a team that had a high level of accountability.
   → Tell the story.

→ What was the effect of being able to count on each other?

→ How did the team achieve that level of accountability?

→ How did you handle conflict?

▰ Each team member needs to be completely committed to saying what he or she will do and doing what he or she says.

→ Just what does that mean for you? Let's go around and answer this: If we have a 2 p.m. phone appointment, what is an acceptable range to call in?

→ Let's go around and talk about what committing to say what we do and do what we say would mean for this team.

▰ I've often heard that the squeaky wheel gets the oil. If that were to be our norm or standard operating procedure, what would it say about us?

→ What effect would that norm have on our productivity?

→ What effect would that norm have on our relationships?

→ What norms can we establish that would eliminate the need for us to squeak for our oil?

→ How can we make it easier for people to be accountable to each other?

▰ Have your ever heard the expression that the operation was a success but the patient died? What does that mean?

→ What would that mean for this project?

→ What can we do to keep ourselves aligned with our target outcome?

→ What can we do to keep each other aligned with our target outcome?

🎬 Let's go around the room and fill in the blank: "If I seem to be off track for achieving (goal), I'd like you to call it to my attention by _____."

→ Who just got permission to have a conversation to help someone get back on track?

→ Are you sincerely ready to receive that level of feedback?

→ Let's affirm that. Walk around the room, and say to each other, "I am committed to supporting you in staying on track through feedback and in allowing you to support me through receiving your feedback."

Perfect Phrases to Break the Ice by Talking about Doubts, Worries, and Concerns

Concerns and doubts can be the elephant in the room. If you don't share them, they can undermine best efforts. These icebreaker phrases address these concerns.

● Is there anything you're concerned about that you'd like to air?

● I don't want to be a buzz kill, but I also don't want to be naïve. I have some concerns I'd like to talk about.

❖ We're laying out an ambitious program here. I'd like to get our doubts and concerns on the table. Those concerns will help us identify problems before they become major obstacles.

❖ We need to address the elephant in the room. We could just ignore him. But we'd still have to clean up the piles of . . . stuff. Let's deal with this now before it gets too deep.

❖ A positive attitude that ignores possible pitfalls is a fool's attitude. The wise imagine what can go wrong, to figure out how to avoid the pitfalls. Where are we vulnerable in this project?

❖ Have you ever been a part of a project where people were afraid to share legitimate doubts, concerns, or worries?
  → What happened?
  → That's why we'll start this (meeting, conversation) talking about doubts and concerns.

 We're stretching. That brings up doubts. If no one has doubts, I'll know we're playing it too safe. So my question is not "Do you have doubts or concerns?" It's "What are they?"
  → Thanks for sharing that. It's amazing how much safer I feel with honest concern than feigned confidence.
  → What can we learn and how can we adapt our approach from understanding the fears?
  → What can we do to realize our dreams instead of our fears?

SECTION 5

WHEN and WHERE: Situation and Location-Based Icebreakers

P laces and circumstances affect how you break the ice. The same group might benefit from a very different opening at a budget meeting compared to a routine staff meeting. Here are icebreaker phrases for the "when" and "where" of icebreaking—based on specific kinds of meetings, events, and exchanges.

Perfect Phrases to Break the Ice at Networking Events

Networking events are one place where you don't need to be subtle about your desire to create business connections. That's what you're there for! So go for it, with these phrases.

- Hi, I'm (give your name), and I'm here to (purpose for your being at the meeting).

- Have you met anyone at these events that you've done business with? Tell me about it.

- Tell me about your business. Why do you do what you do?

- What is the best part of your business?

- How is your business affected by this economy?

- How did you get into your business?

- What would you tell someone just starting out in your business?

- What kind of business contacts are you looking for at these events?

- I'm on the lookout for (example: a virtual admin). If you meet one, can you let me know?

- Last time I came to one of these events, I met (professional) who helped me (project). Have you made some great connections at these things?

- I have a 30-second elevator speech about what I do. Are you ready?

❖ We're going to circulate for a while. Today I give you permission to tell people the exact reason you're here and what kind of connections you're looking for.

▰ Before I turn you loose to network, we're going to create meaningful greetings to use with each other. "Hi, how are you?" won't fly.

  → As a table, discuss and decide on five greetings that come across as genuine and help move the conversation forward. Something like, "I'd like to learn more about your business," or "What's it like in your industry these days?"

→ Time. Now mingle.
→ How did the exercise influence your opening?
→ Who found a new greeting that really helped them connect with someone?

Perfect Phrases to Break the Ice at Professional and Industry Gatherings

Too many people miss the opportunity of industry gatherings. You're not just there to hear the speakers and visit the displays. You're there to meet and connect with other industry professionals. These phrases will help break the ice.

● Have you heard any of the speakers before? Who did you come to hear?

● What is the most useful thing you've learned so far?

● What are you hoping to learn from this (trade show, conference, meeting)?

● I'm from (your location). Did you travel far to get here?

● I'm planning my agenda. What sessions are you attending?

● Are you enjoying the (trade show, conference, meeting)? What are you getting out of it?

● I come to these things because I see the industry from the perspective of (example: writer, vendor). I like to see it from many different angles. How about you?

● Aside from me, ☺ who are some of the interesting people you've met here?

● I don't believe in having lunch, or dinner, or even breakfast alone! Would you like to join me?

- What brings you to this (trade show, conference, meeting)?

- I've already met so many people! How do you keep track of your contacts from these events?

- This is my first time here. How about you?

- What other industry conferences do you attend?

❖ As a presenter at industry conferences, I once had someone write on the evaluation that they learned more from the other attendees at my session than from me. I actually considered that a positive comment. This session is about (topic, skill). It's not about me. I don't care where you get your ahas. I just care that you get them.

🎬 We did a review of registrations and found that we have (number) industries represented here. My challenge for you is to get at least one business card from someone in each of the industries. We'll check in at every general session for updates on how we're doing.

→ How many of you have cards from 10 different industries so far? Twenty, anyone?

Perfect Phrases to Break the Ice at Office Socials

What do you say to someone you have an all-business relationship with, or no relationship with, when you meet at an office social? Here are some phrases.

- We haven't met before. What department do you work in?
  → I'm in (department). Any messages for me and my team?

→ This is supposed to be a social. Do you mind if I cheat a little and ask a few questions about your department?

● I don't think we've met, but I might have forgotten. Have we?
  → Do you ever forget people's faces too?
  → I once forgot (example: the CEO). That was awkward!
  → Do you have any tips or tricks for remembering names?

● Your face is so familiar, but your name has slipped my mind. Can you refresh my memory?

● I've worked with you for years and don't know a thing about you! I'm not sure where to start, but just to get it going, what do you think about the latest policy to (policy)?

● Man, this is going to be a challenge! This is supposed to be a social, and I'm so tempted to talk shop. Do me a favor, will you, and tug my sleeve if I slip and start talking business with you?

● It's really different to be putting a face to the e-mails we've exchanged. It's a whole new dimension. Are you surprised by what any of us looks like?

❖ OK, heads up. This is a social, got it? Anyone caught talking shop doesn't get ice cream.

Perfect Phrases to Break the Ice at Industry Parties

Remember, a party is a party. Even if it's a party of industry professionals, shake it up a bit and have some fun.

- I've been wondering how (example: CPAs) party at their conferences. Now I know!

- You know what's unique about (industry; example: health professional) parties? It's the only group I know that (example: serves digestive enzymes with the meal).

- I love it when (example: office professionals) throw a party because they know how to (example: cover all the details).

- The entertainment committee did a great job! Do you know who was on it?

- This decor is marvelous! I really love the (specific).

- Have you ever seen seven Elvises on one stage before?

- Check it out! This group cleans up well! Is this the same group I attended sessions with earlier?

❖ This is a party, so focus on fun and play. If you find yourself compelled to talk shop with anyone, take it outside. Kidding about that—but let the merriment begin.

Perfect Phrases to Break the Ice at Lunch and Dinner Meetings

Breaking bread together is a time-honored way to build business relationships. These phrases will help you create warmth in your meeting.

- Sometimes I get so excited talking about business I forget to eat. I look down, and my plate is full when everyone else's is empty. Does that happen to you?

● I like meeting over (lunch, dinner). I can tell if I'm talking too much if your plate is empty while mine is still full.

● This is a great/charming/elegant restaurant. Where else do you like to eat?

● The menu looks overwhelming/unfamiliar/interesting. Do you have any recommendations?

● I thought a (lunch, dinner) meeting would be a relaxing environment to talk about our next steps.

● Do you remember when eating out was special? I remind myself of that so I can appreciate it.

● I wanted to get away from the office to talk over (topic). Something about food makes it easier to exchange ideas.

● Don't mess with me, or I might start a food fight! ☺

❖ Before we get down to business, I'd like to make a toast (water glasses are fine).
   → To work. May we never be without it.
   → To our company. May we keep it profitable.
   → To the project. May we end on schedule and within budget, or if not, at least have good excuses! *Really* kidding on that last point.

🎬 Since we're meeting over dinner, we'll start with a simple icebreaker. Please turn to the person across the table and tell him or her where you work and what your main project is these days.

Perfect Phrases to Break the Ice at Board Meetings

Ideally, board meetings are gatherings of enthusiastic professionals with a common interest. They meet to share their expertise to further a cause or mission. In reality, sometimes they are gatherings of overworked professionals who wonder why they ever agreed to serve, or judgmental stakeholders who are convinced everything will work out just fine if only people would listen to them. In any case, here are phrases to break the ice.

❖ I told my friend I had a board meeting to go to, and she thought that sounded glamorous. I'll pause for laughter before I continue.

❖ I told my daughter I had a board meeting, and she looked confused. She thought I was talking about the other kind of bored. It's an old joke, but it still happens.

❖ We sent out a preview of today's agenda so you could prepare. Who had time to review it?

❖ The last several fund-raisers have been both successful and learning events. What brought our successes? How could we do even better?

❖ We have challenges to address today, but let's begin by giving a round of appreciation to the conference (or other appropriate focus) committee. Wow, what a success!

❖ Let's begin by sharing any breakthroughs or celebrations since our last meeting. Who has one?

❖ Welcome to our new board members. Let's start with tips from other board members on how to join in smoothly.

Perfect Phrases to Break the Ice at Business Meetings

All things being equal, people like doing business with their friends. All things not being equal, people like doing business with their friends. Business meetings are about business, and you can irritate the task-oriented with your questions about where they're from or who their favorite musician is. But making conversation a bit more personal can make it more like you're doing business with your friends—even if you just met.

- I've been looking forward to meeting with you because (example: I've admired your work for years).

- We finally meet again! What's your biggest news since we last met?

- We have a lot to cover in a little time, so I know you want to get down to business like I do. I do want to tell you how much I appreciate your taking the time to meet me.

- I am so excited about this opportunity; my assistant had to peel me off the ceiling! I'm ready to dive into details if you are.

❖ Let's run this meeting according to (your name)'s Rules of Order: Be brief. Be respectful. Be outta here. Sound right?

▰ Let's go around the room and update each other. We'll start by sharing the best thing that happened since we last met.

🎬 Just to make sure that we all know each other, let's go around the room and quickly introduce ourselves with our names and our positions. And, briefly add what you hope to get out of the meeting.

Perfect Phrases to Break the Ice at Association Meetings

By definition, you have things in common with people in your associations. They travel a related or parallel path as yours. Think about common experiences and challenges you have when preparing to break the ice with association members.

● I joined this association because (example: the industry is changing so quickly I thought it would help me keep up). How has being a member helped you professionally?

● I heard about this association through a client. How did you find out about it?

● How has being a part of this association helped your business?

● What part of this business are you in?

● Any tips for a newcomer about how to get the most out of this association?

● What made you decide to join this association?

● You'll like this association because (benefit).

● The best thing about this association for me is (benefit).

● Are there things about this association I might not know about?

● Do you volunteer for this association? What do you do?

● I joined this association as (example: a vendor to the profession). How about you?

❖ As members of (association), we are associated by our interest in (association purpose). During our breaks, I invite you to find out why your fellow attendees are here.

❖ Let's start this association meeting by sharing stories of how we've benefited from association meetings. This will be a table discussion.

➔ Now let's do a second round. This time, talk about what you do to make connections and get value out of these meetings. How do you mingle, make connections, and form relationships?

➔ Sometimes we hear that people stop coming to meetings because they don't get value from them. We're always racking our brains to figure out how to help you connect. We can only do so much. The rest is up to you.

Perfect Phrases to Break the Ice at Conferences

Conferences have a lot in common with association meetings. In fact, many conferences also are association meetings. The difference tends to be in the size—conferences are bigger—and the frequency—conferences are less frequent.

I like to think of fellow conference participants as shared explorers on the great adventure of learning what's going on in the world of whatever the conference is for. Think about that when you design your own icebreakers.

- Have you learned anything yet?
  → What?
  → How do you expect to apply that?
- I'm starting to hit the conference coma. How about you?
- What stood out for you most here today?
- I'm excited to be here because (reason). How about you?
- Have you figured out how to get your name tag on right? I tend to fumble with them.
- What's the most interesting thing you've learned so far?
- Is there any session you wouldn't miss for anything?
- My brain is stuffed! I'm looking for someone to eat with and talk about anything else. Interested?
- What's your strategy for getting the most out of conferences?
- ❖ Remember, one of the greatest values of attending conferences is the connections you make. Think of people in the rooms and halls with you as potential gold mines of support and information. How do you extract the gold?

Perfect Phrases to Break the Ice at Training Events

Training events are the birthplace of icebreakers. People need to feel safe and like to feel connected to learn. Then they're more willing to take risks, to participate, and to ask questions. Great training icebreakers bring a group of strangers into acquaintances and short-term friendships.

If you don't find the icebreaker you're looking for here, check out the table of contents. Most sections have at least one phrase or activity that could be used at a training event.

❖ I find that at training sessions, the people who ask the most questions generally are the most knowledgeable already. I like that, and frankly, I don't think it's a coincidence. So the first person to ask a considered question gets a prize.

❖ Training is an event. Learning is a process. Today is an event that will start an ongoing process.

❖ I'm (name), and I know everything there is to know about (topic). And if you believe that, today will be far less interesting. I do have a great program for you, and my program combined with our shared knowledge should make for a great day.

❖ Let's start out with what everyone wants to know, like where are the bathrooms? And when are the breaks?

❖ They say we remember 90 percent of what we do and only 10 percent of what we hear. That's why we'll be creating a lot of experiences and having hands-on practice today.

▰ Let's introduce ourselves by telling our fortunes. Share what you do now, and then share what you will be doing in five years. For example, you might say, right now I'm assistant to the director of operations. When I look into the future, I see myself in the same position, but handling more of my manager's responsibilities. Let's start.

▰ Please write down three things you want to walk away knowing how to do from this training.

  → Now tell your table what your three things are.

→ Now please write your desires on a sticky note and place it on the flip chart up front.

→ When your goal is met, please take your note down. You can do it during the session or on breaks. Of course, if you do it during a session, we're likely to ask you to tell us about it.

→ Why do you suppose I asked you to go through all these steps? What's the value?

🎬 I'd like you to discover something you have in common with the people at your table.

→ Please share what you learned.

→ Now break off in pairs. I'd like for you to discover something unusual you have in common with your partner.

→ What did you find? (Go around.)

→ Is the thing you discovered in common with the person you were paired with more personal than what you discovered with the table?

→ How did it feel to realize you had that in common?

Perfect Phrases to Break the Ice at New Employee Orientation—Employers

You can do an impersonal employee orientation and be effective. But icebreakers that really make the new employee (or new employees) feel welcome will have an added benefit of creating an environment where the employee feels comfortable making sure his or her questions are answered.

● Well, I was new once, and I know what I wanted to know and needed to know and what they told me at orientation.

There was a difference! I'm committed to telling you both what you want to know and what you need to know.

● You have no idea how happy we are to have you on board here. Here's my orientation request: speak up if I am not telling you what you need to learn here. Deal?

● If I say something that you don't understand, ask me to explain—especially if I break into alphabet soup! We use a lot of acronyms around here, and we forget we're doing it.

❖ Anybody feeling disoriented? Sounds like orientation is the perfect place for you to be!

🎬 You'll be meeting the longtimers soon, but for now, I invite you to turn to your neighbor and introduce yourself and tell him or her about your expertise and experience.

🎬 As new employees, you have a lot to learn about the people and places in our company. You won't learn everything in one day, but every experience will increase your knowledge. To help you start building that knowledge in a fun way, we're going to have a scavenger hunt! You'll pair up and find items or answers to questions. Feel free to ask anyone for help. Don't worry, the other departments know you're coming! The winning team members will each receive (some silly reward). Everyone has to be back here by (time). Find a partner, and come up and get your scavenger list!

→ What was the most interesting thing you learned?

→ I'd like to hear some of your strategies. How did you approach the scavenger hunt?

🎬 You all have the orientation packet. I'm going to give you a little time to go through it, individually. Then, we'll divide into two teams, and each team will come up with 10 questions to ask the other team. So, as you're reading individually, you can try to think of some good questions. Of course, you can't ask a question unless you know the answer!

→ I wonder if some of our longtime employees would have been able to answer some of those questions!

→ How did this process help you learn the material?

→ How could you apply this process in your jobs?

Perfect Phrases to Break the Ice at New Employee Orientation—Employees

How about if you're the new employee? Your orientation should be planned well enough that you don't need to fumble for words. Still, it helps to prepare.

● It's been so long since I started a new job, I'm not sure what to ask.

● I'm excited to be working here because (example: you have the state of the art technology).

● It's my first day, and that means there's no such thing as a dumb question, right?

● When I'm new, I like to start by observing and getting a feel for the way things work before I ask a lot of questions or give advice. Sound right?

● I want to learn everything I can as fast as I can to get up to speed as soon as I can. You'll let me know if I'm asking too many questions, won't you?

● I'll be open about what I don't know. That's how I can learn quickly.

Perfect Phrases to Break the Ice at Routine Staff Meetings

Why would you need an icebreaker at a routine staff meeting? Well, you're reading this section, so chances are you have your own reasons. Think about them before you read ours.

Routine staff meetings can become rote and impersonal. Even if familiarity hasn't bred contempt, it can have a way of building up walls and barriers that no one even notices. These phrases will break those walls down.

❖ OK, this is a routine staff meeting. How can we shake it up a bit to make sure we're in a routine and not a rut?

→ Do you know the difference between a routine and a rut? If we do things a certain way that leads to progress, it's a routine. If not, it's a rut.

→ The only differences between a rut and a grave are the depth of the hole and the length of the stay. Time to make sure our rut doesn't become a grave.

→ What ruts might we be in?

→ What have you done at routine meetings to keep them from becoming ruts?

❖ Let's add variety to our meeting by having someone else lead it. Who's up for that?

❖ Today is backwards day. We'll follow our agenda—backwards. We'll start with the action steps, move to the discussion, and then on to the reports.

🎬 When we see each other regularly, it's easy to assume we know what's going on with each other. Let's go around and talk about what's not routine for us these days before we dive into our routine meeting.

→ Any surprises?

Perfect Phrases to Break the Ice at Intermittent Meetings

Intermittent meetings can be like drinking from a fire hose. Usually the meeting has a very specific purpose, and yet if you haven't had regular meetings, there could be a huge backlog of topics to cover, issues to raise, and problems to solve. People can feel like they're drowning in a flood of information. These phrases can help.

❖ It's great to get you all in one room again. Since we don't get to meet very often, we'll want to make good use of our time. But first—Hi! Welcome! Hooray! You're here!

❖ Ya know, meeting irregularly like we do is like drinking from a fire hose. Anyone else with me on that?

❖ A lot has happened since we last met. I bet I don't know the half of it. So here's the deal. We have a goal for this meeting which is (goal). As we move forward toward that goal, if any one of us says something that indicates we've been out of the loop on something, we'll stop and catch up and then move forward. Agreed?

❖ It seems like it's been ages since we last met! I almost feel like it's the first day of school after a long summer. What interesting experiences have you had since our last meeting?

❖ Let's start this meeting on a positive note. What good has happened since our last meeting?

❖ It's been so long since our last meeting, I feel like I need to reintroduce everyone! I think some of us have grown a few inches it's been so long! Or lost a few inches . . .

🎬 In a perfect world, we'd meet every (day, week, month). In our world, we meet whenever we have a crisis. We need to focus. But before we do that, let's do an icebreaker so we don't just see each other in terms of our problems.

→ Break into pairs, and complete the following sentence. If this weren't a meeting about (crisis) I'd want to talk about _____.

→ Who shared or heard a topic that we all should hear?

Perfect Phrases to Break the Ice at Procedural Update Meetings

Procedural update meetings sound like a real snore—and generally they are. They can also be a real hotbed of upset—you're messing with people's habits! No matter how well considered, your procedural changes are likely to inconvenience someone somehow. These phrases will help.

❖ Life as you knew it is over. I'm kidding—but we have made a few procedural changes.

❖ We figure you're just about used to the last procedural changes we made, so it's time for some new ones. Kidding!

❖ I'm about to ask you to do one of the hardest things anyone can do: change a habit. We have procedural updates for you.

❖ Let's begin by standing up and stretching a bit. Why? Because then we're going to sit down and stretch a lot. We have some new procedures that will be a stretch for most of us at first. On your feet!

❖ We have changes to announce. Don't let us close this meeting without telling you the reason for each and why they're both necessary and beneficial.

🎬 Let's open by crossing our arms like this.

→ Now fold your arms with the opposite one on top. Some of us can't even do it!

→ We're about to introduce some procedural changes that will be like folding our arms "backwards." Trust me, they will get easier! Just to prove that change is possible, let me brag a moment. I can cross my arms either way! Are you impressed?

🎬 I'm going to ask you four questions, and I want you to answer in unison. Are you ready?

→ (Hold up document printed on white paper.) What color paper is this printed on?

→ What do cows drink?

→ Actually, cows drink water. Notice how you unconsciously said "milk" without really thinking about it?

→ OK, I set it up that way. I told you there would be four questions, and that got you thinking ahead. Plus my paper is white and milk is white and your unconscious mind made the association and said, "don't worry, honey, I've got this one handled." Just like I set you up, life sets us up too. We'll find ourselves unconsciously reverting to old procedures if we don't stay alert.

→ So here are the new procedures. Let's support each other in implementing them.

Perfect Phrases to Break the Ice at Budget Meetings

Like procedural meetings, budget meetings can be boring and they can also be highly contentious. Many department heads, managers, and other professionals have learned to pad their budgets to have something to negotiate down from. That pressures the rest of the team to do likewise, and before you know it, colleagues who should be collaborating are operating as adversaries. "I need the FTE more than you do!"

The best icebreakers at budget meetings remind the attendees of the shared mission and of the need to balance individual needs and the overall purpose.

❖ I've been to budget meetings where people fought for their own interests instead of for the greater good, and where people took it personally when their requests were declined, and where people tried to increase the perceived value of their projects (budget needs, etc.) by tearing others down. So I admit, I'm a little apprehensive about today. I've also been to budget meetings where people worked together to allocate resources and come up with some really creative solutions. I'd like today to be the second kind of budget meeting.

❖ We're here to divide a budget pie. No one ever thinks his or her piece of the pie is big enough. Or at least we never admit it when we do. I'm hoping today will be an exception.

❖ You each know why your projects are important. You each represent a piece of the pie. We'll hear what you honestly need and why, and consider it in light of everything. Please work with us so we can make the larger decisions reasonably.

▰ Let's start by sharing our stories of budget meetings that have gone really well—where people worked together to allocate resources in the most productive ways.
  → What was it like?
  → What did people do differently?
  → What made it work?
  → What can we do here today to make this budget meeting operate like the ones we just heard about?

Perfect Phrases to Break the Ice at Strategic Meetings

Strategic meetings require creativity and decisiveness. Set the stage to invite both.

❖ We know the "what." It's time to figure out the "how." Let's keep revisiting the "what" when we look at the "how."

❖ Today, we need to set aside our day-to-day challenges and to focus on high-level issues. Where we're going and what we need to do to get there.

❖ Before we get too involved in where we want to go, let's review where we've been and how we got there. What strategies worked well? What strategies didn't work?

❖ This isn't just another meeting. This is our opportunity to envision and take the first steps toward a different future for our organization.

❖ I'm sure you've heard the phrase, "The hand that rocks the cradle is the hand that rules the world." Our organization is the cradle. You are the hands.

❖ Have you ever watched a house being built? It's just a hole in the ground for a long time and then all of a sudden the framework goes up and it's done. Most of the time and effort was spent on the foundation. The foundation is the most important part. Today we are going to do foundational work for our organization.

Perfect Phrases to Break the Ice at New Team Formation Meetings

New team formation is a discovery process. People have apprehensions. They anticipate what's to come. They're jockeying for position, finding their alliances, and feeling out the new situation. These phrases will help.

❖ We're tasked with an important project. As you know, our company mission is to (mission). To help us achieve that, we're forming this team to (project). This is important because (reason).

❖ Problems often drive greatness. I know I'm not the only one who is bugged by the way we (complaint, problem, issue). Well, we get to do something about it.

❖ I'm excited about this team and the project we're tasked with because (reason).

❖ This project is important to our organization because (reason).

❖ I imagine we're all looking around wondering, what the heck did I get myself into here? Who's in this sandbox with me?

❖ This reminds me of the first day of school when I looked around and wondered who was in my class. It's kind of like getting a peek into the future and what it's likely to be like.

❖ I've found that new teams like to know what the work is first. So let's start there. Then we can get to know each other.

❖ Look around. These are the people you will be depending on for your success, and they're the people who will be depending on you. Let's start with a discussion about how we can create the trust we need to function effectively.

🎬 Let's start by breaking into groups of two and introducing ourselves to each other. Then I'll ask you to introduce your partner to the team as a whole.

🎬 Here's a funny way to remember my name. (Some word association with your name.) Let's go around the team and give each other ways to remember our names.

🎬 Let's go around the team and fill in the blanks:

→ My personal accomplishments that I'm proudest of are _____.

→ My professional accomplishments that I'm proudest of are _____.

→ Some unique skills and experiences I bring to this team are _____.

→ My expectations and hopes for this team are _____.

🎬 A great thing about strong teams is that we tend to get right to business. Before we do that today, let's break some ice by introducing team members.

→ I'll start by introducing everyone and listing skills that led to their selection to the team. Then we'll introduce ourselves and add any additional skills that I might have overlooked.

🎬 Discussion question: What are the key distinctions between a team, a group, and a committee?

→ What makes us a team and not a group?

🎬 Since we don't all know each other, let's take a few minutes to learn more about each other. But rather than have you introduce yourselves, I'd like you to introduce another team member. I'll give you a few minutes to pair up and talk before you introduce each other. Find out the other person's name, his or her title, and an accomplishment that's *not* work-related.

→ What an interesting bunch we are!

→ You guys did a great job on our first team project!

→ Should we have signed confidentiality agreements? Anything too revealing?

Perfect Phrases to Break the Ice Online

Breaking the ice and building rapport virtually, through online social networking, e-mail, conference calls, and video, has emerged as the first contact method for many. The good news is that most of the in-person icebreaker phrases work online as well. However, the icebreakers typically need to be shorter (especially e-mail subject lines), and words alone often need to convey an entire message, without body language or tone of voice.

Connecting through online social networking—LinkedIn (contacts), Facebook (friends), Twitter (followers), and so on— including internal organizational networks, involves finding commonality: a person, an interest, a group, an event, a website, an article, a posting. Include a personal message when you ask to connect. You can mention a mutual connection and give an honest reason as to why you want to connect. You also can comment on or retweet a posting to begin to develop rapport. Hanging around a blogger's site and posting occasionally is valuable too. In the online world, there is little need for chitchat on first contact.

- Hi, I'm a (friend, business associate, coworker) of (mutual contact). I'd like to connect because (reason).

- I read your (blog, article) on (topic) and found it really useful because (reason).

- Hi, I notice that we (share an interest in, like, work for, lived in, went to school at, are members of . . .). I'd love to connect to talk about that.

- I like what you had to say in (source) about (subject), and I'd like to add your feed to my wall. I post on (example: communication skills and technology). Would you add me as a friend?

- Hi, I notice that you (will be attending, work at) (place) and I'd love to connect with some people before I get there.

- You keep popping up on my (LinkedIn, Facebook), so I thought we should get connected. I like to be deliberate and purposeful in my networking, and I think we could share our ideas well.

- (Mutual contact) just joined my network on LinkedIn, and I would like to invite you to join it, too.

- We met at (place) (yesterday, last month, etc.). I really enjoyed talking with you about (topic). I'd like to keep in touch and add you (as a friend, to my professional network).

- Hi, I'm writing a (book, article, blog post) on (topic) and would love to connect with you about that.

Summary and Conclusion

Writing this has been a fun journey for Diane and me. The concept started with one vision and continued to evolve. We hope its final evolution is useful to you. Pick and choose. There are some icebreakers here Diane would never use, and there are icebreakers here I would never use. At least we think we wouldn't. I say that because some icebreakers we initially resisted have since grown on us.

In the opening, we used the icebreaker of "If you were an animal, which one would you be" as an example of a trite meeting opener. Since then, a colleague told me how she uses it effectively at high-level business meetings. Then, out of the blue my own husband started talking about what animal he would be if given a choice. It was an interesting conversation.

So if an icebreaker doesn't hit you right, stay open to it. It might surprise you. You never know. Some of us have effectively broken the ice talking about how ineffective an icebreaker is.

If you appreciate the irony of that observation, Diane and I expect you'll never be at a loss for how to break the ice again.

APPENDIX

Phrases to Find Partners and Form Groups

This is a phrase book to break the ice when you open a conversation, meeting, or presentation. Some of the phrases introduce ice-breaking activities that require a partner. This section gives you phrases to help your listeners find partners and form groups whether you're at the beginning, middle, or end of a meeting or presentation. It also gives phrases to decide who leads or goes first. There are some very fun ways to do that.

❖ Hand out playing cards. Find people with the same suit card you have.

❖ Hand out playing cards. Form groups based on the numbers on the cards. Aces together please! Kings, queens, and jacks, find each other. Same goes for the rest of the deck.

❖ We're going to play different roles for the first part of the meeting. You have cards that determine your role.

→ Hearts are (role; example: advocates). Your role is to . . .

→ Clubs are (role; example: opponents). Your mission is to . . .

→ Diamonds are (role). Your mission is to . . .

→ Spades are (role). I want you to . . .

→ Aces and Jokers are wild. You can play any role you want.

❖ Form groups based on the season you were born in. January to March, form over there. April to June, you're meeting there. July to September in the other corner. October to December, that part of the room is for you.

❖ We're going to form groups based on your birth month. Circulate while repeating your birth month. So if it were me, I'd circulate saying, "November! November!"

❖ Raise your right hand if you were born in an even-numbered month: February, April, June, August, October, or December.

→ Keep your right hand where it is. Now raise your left hand if you were born on an even-numbered day.

→ If both hands are up, you're an A.

→ If both hands are down, you're a B.

→ If your right hand is up and your left is down, you're a C.

→ If your left hand is up and your right hand is down, you're a D.

❖ I've handed out slips of paper with common pairs. Find your opposite. Salt? Find your pepper. Hot? Find your cold. Go.

❖ Think of a number between 1 and 50. Got it? OK. If it's even, go over there. If it's odd, go there.

❖ Mingle until I blow the whistle.

   Whomever you're talking with now is your partner for this exercise.

❖ Let's count off. 1, 2, 3, 4, 1, 2, 3, 4, and so on.

   Now find your matching numbers.

❖ The person with the lightest-colored hair goes first.

   → The person with the most hair on their head goes first.

   → The person who has been here the longest goes first.

   → The (taller, tallest) person goes first.

❖ Everyone, raise your hand and point to the ceiling.

   → On three, point to the person you vote to lead.

   → Got it? Now, if you were chosen, delegate your role out now, if you like.

About the Authors

Meryl Runion is a Certified Speaking Professional and the creator of the SpeakSTRONG Method of Communication. Her 10 books provide PowerPhrases that help professionals say what they mean and mean what they say without being mean when they say it. Meryl's books have sold more than 350,000 copies worldwide. She lives in Cascade, Colorado, where she hikes, dances, and helps people figure out how to say things. You can reach her at www.speakstrong.com.

Diane Windingland is a professional speaker and the author of *Small Talk, Big Results: Chit Chat Your Way to Success!* As an engineer, salesperson, wife and mother, and karate instructor, she brings a broad range of roles into her training and writing about small talk and breaking the ice. Diane lives in St. Paul, Minnesota. You can reach Diane at www.smalltalkbigresults.com.

The Right Phrase for Every Situation...Every Time.

THE IDEAL PERFORMANCE SUPPORT SOLUTION FOR MANAGERS AND SUPERVISORS

With over 30,000 phrases, *Perfect Phrases for Managers* is an unmatched digital resource that provides managers at every level with the skills they need to effectively manage any situation.

From performance reviews to documenting problems, to motivating and coaching teams, to managing difficult people and embarrassing situations, this performance support tool will help your company create an environment for exceptional performance.

Go to **www.perfectphrases.com** to learn more about *Perfect Phrases for Managers* and how you can access:

- A "Things to Consider" section with hundreds of bite-size coaching tips
- Audio clips from actual conversations
- Strategies for opening up healthy communication

The right phrase for every situation, every time.

Visit www.perfectphrases.com to learn how your company can qualify for a trial subscription.

31901051120816